"God's Timeline is an ideal text or resource for Christian universities and seminaries. Rev. Rick's storytelling style models that of Jesus, the Master Teacher. His use of the timeline of Christ's redemptive work throughout Scripture and beyond gives His story thematic coherence that I have not seen accomplished to this extent before. The Integrative Questions in each chapter and the companion Teacher's Guide is pedagogy at its very best. This is a must-read for both believers and those exploring the faith."

—JAMES J. JUERGENSEN
Director of Graduate Studies
Concordia University, Wisconsin

"Christianity lives by a confession, namely, the confession that 'Jesus is Lord.' Pastor Meyer perceptively notes that this confession presupposes a story and makes little sense apart from that story. Thus Meyer sets out to tell that story (what he calls 'God's Timeline') in a compelling and fresh way for a culture that no longer knows God's grand story from creation to the 'Ultimate Restoration' of creation. He succeeds admirably in this task. In the process, he shows us where and how we fit into God's story and helps us to discover the purpose of our lives on earth. This book will be a tremendous resource for pastors and congregations who would introduce people to the Christian story and with it the Christian life of faith and hope."

—CHARLES P. ARAND
Professor of Systematic Theology
Concordia Seminary, St. Louis

God's Timeline

God's Timeline

An Introduction to Theology for Laypeople

RICK MEYER

WIPF & STOCK · Eugene, Oregon

Wifp & Stock
An imprint of Wipf and Stock Publishers
199 W. 8th Ave., Suite 3
Eugene, OR 97401

www.wipfandstock.com

ISBN 13: 978-1-62032-599-5

Manufactured in the U.S.A.

To my amazing wife, DeAnne,
and my beautiful daughters, Elizabeth and Emily

Contents

Acknowledgments

I AM INDEBTED TO those who have shared in the study of God's Word with me over the last 30 years. In addition I want to thank my dear friend Jim Ware, who kindly read the early manuscript and provided invaluable feedback. The book is much better because of it.

Also, a special thank you to my daughter, Elizabeth, for the illustrations.

Foreword

"IN THE BEGINNING GOD said." "In the beginning was the Word." The Creator of all that exists likes to talk. He reveals himself as a God of conversation and community. As he reports what he thinks and what he has done and is doing in the Bible, he is always connecting with his human creatures in conversation and building community with them through that conversation.

God has left traces of his creative Word all around us, in nature, in human experience, in human sensitivity to what is right and wrong in daily life. But when we try to engage him apart from the Word he has given us through his chosen prophets and apostles—those who proclaim his message, those whom he has sent with his Word—we usually find ourselves in conversation with ourselves. We are dependent on his approach to us. We are dependent on his addressing us. We are dependent on his initiating the conversation through Holy Scripture.

The prophets of the Old Testament and the apostles and evangelists of the New Testament have left behind a relatively small book. Dickens and Tolstoy have left us a good deal more words than are in the Bible. But God has given us in the words of the prophets and the apostles all we need to know about him. His Holy Spirit did not have a textbook written. God is a storyteller. He has designed his human creatures not as static, unmoving creatures, but as people, in his image, who are always on the move through the passage of time. The prophets and the apostles unfold God's story in Scripture in historical settings, as God moved with his chosen people, Israel first, then his church, along a timeline he draws from Creation to Ultimate Restoration.

Because the Bible presents this moving history of God's actions in his world and his inter-actions with his human creatures, we often encounter difficulties in finding the golden thread that ties the story together when we plunge into its message at any given place. Because that is true, the people of God have always formulated summaries of the biblical message for teaching their children, for recalling themselves the goodness of God, for giving witness to their faith and to its center, the second person of the Holy Trinity, Jesus of Nazareth, the Messiah. God's people have *ech*oed in what Christians have called "cat*eche*sis" the basic foundations of God's revelation of himself in Scripture through brief summaries of the heart of their faith. Such summaries remind us of the goodness of our God. They remind us of the basics which our children need to hear. They offer us the foundations in which new Christians build their lives and their view of reality under our guidance.

Pastor Rick Meyer has spent a quarter of a century studying God's Word in the context of thinking about the needs of the people of God and of those who stand outside the community that God has created as his church. He has lived and thought and spoken between the poles of God's Word and the real needs of real people caught in the midst of a world that brings both blessings and curses, good days and terrible days, to those surrounded by evils of all kinds. Pastor Meyer has practiced the art of helping people turn from false gods to listen to God speaking through the Scriptures. He has exercised countless times the responsibility of bringing human beings into conversation and community with their Creator, their Redeemer, Jesus Christ, and the Holy Spirit.

In this volume Pastor Meyer continues the conversation that God has initiated and mediates through his people with you, the reader, and those to whom God sends you to speak. Pastor Meyer brings you through the Scripture with a voice that effectively echoes its main themes and gives you an overview of God's marching and strolling through the cultures and crowds in which his people have been testifying to his love in Christ for centuries.

God speaks with us in a covenantal promise, Pastor Meyer reminds us, creating the community that rests upon his love and expresses itself in our trust in him. He will bring you into the biblical text in these pages in such a way that you will clearly see the structure of God's movement from Creation through our rebellion and doubt that have separated us from God, toward the Ultimate Restoration of his creation when the risen Jesus Christ returns at the end of time as we know it.

Because God's people, from the Passover of old to the present day, have taught their faith with questions and answers, Pastor Meyer poses "integrative questions" designed to make this conversation with the biblical writers alive and penetrating right into the core of our thinking and planning and evaluating our own daily existence. His guidance through Israel's history highlights what God was up to as he proclaimed himself and his will for his people through the prophets. His sober assessment of human sin will lead readers to reflect on their own experiences as victims and as perpetrators of our common rebellion against our Maker. His embrace of Jesus as our Savior and Lord will infect readers with the sense of the love that Christ showed us as he died and rose to make us fully human again.

It is all about words since words are what God has chosen as the instrument of his power and presence, his way of creating conversation and community between himself and his human creatures. Thus, at the end of this book a handy glossary provides a reference work to which readers can turn again and again.

It is always an adventure to get into conversation with God. This book will lead you into that conversation and drive you to reply in prayer to the Holy Trinity, Father, Son, and Holy Spirit. It will lead you to recall how good God has been, especially in his coming to die and rise for us as Jesus of Nazareth. And it will lead you to teach those around you more of the faith you share with them—and also to give witness to God and his Word as you walk through this little part of God's history with those who do not yet know him. What an adventure God's Word is.

Robert Kolb
Concordia Seminary, Saint Louis
The Sixteenth Sunday after Pentecost 2012

To The Reader

IF YOU WOULD LIKE to download a complete Teacher's Guide for this book, please go to *meyerbooks.com* to access this helpful tool.

Also, if you are reading this book as part of a study group or class and would like for me to visit your group to discuss it with you, I would welcome your invitation. While I cannot travel to be with you in person, the technologies of Skype and conference calling have provided us with the next best thing. Please feel free to contact me at rickmeyerbooks@sbcglobal.net to set up a visit with your group. (Make sure to put the letters GTL in the subject line of your email.)

Rick Meyer

Introduction

OVER THE PAST THIRY-PLUS years, I have often searched for a theological framework or foundation upon which I could construct a clear understanding of Scripture. I have longed for some type of model or structure into which the pieces of doctrine would fit to form a coherent whole. Unfortunately, I have never found anything that really satisfied my need. While catechisms and other creedal statements have been extremely helpful, they have still left me without a way to see how everything is related.

I am so thankful that my frustrations have not become a deterrent in my quest to see Scripture as a whole. In fact, quite the opposite has been the case. It seems that God has given me just enough light to see the next piece and its relatedness so that I would keep looking for more. But how many people have had the opportunities to learn what I have? Or how many would-be students of the Bible have simply given up and concluded that the Bible is just too difficult to comprehend? More troubling perhaps is the question of how many people have become susceptible to every wind of doctrine that blows because of a poorly formed foundation.

This book is my attempt to meet a need. I want to provide a foundation, a framework, a picture of how Scripture holds together. Like a house that can't be built until there is a foundation and frame, my desire is for the student of Scripture to see the most important, foundational parts of God's Word and how they relate to one another. The goal of this effort is to give the reader confidence in understanding the whole so that when individual parts (or doctrines) come up, the student of the Word has a clear sense of where those parts fit.

The design of this book lends itself to be used as a tool for pastors and lay leaders who want to teach a foundational class in theology, as well as for individuals and small groups who want to learn on their own. The material in this book will be beneficial for those new to the faith and for those who have been in the church for many years. The Integrative Questions at the end of each chapter (starting with chapter 2) will strengthen the student's understanding and comprehension of the material. And the Glossary of Terms at the end will not only support the study of this book, but can also be used as a stand-alone tool for review and deeper learning.

The Bible is not an easy book to read and fully comprehend. Oh, the most basic message of salvation can be found in numerous places. But the Bible as a whole is a very challenging book (or library of books). Consequently, it is necessary for us to have a good foundation and framework upon which to build our knowledge of God's Word as we continue to study and learn throughout the entirety of our lives.

The writer of the Letter to the Hebrews challenged his readers to become teachers of God's Word. Apparently, the original audience for this letter had been taught the basics of the Christian faith, but had lost sight of their need to dig deeper and grow to the point that they would be able to teach others what they had learned. Consequently, the author of Hebrews developed his message so that the hearers could see how what happened in the Old Testament was preparatory for the first coming (or "appearing," as most New Testament references put it) of Christ.

In many ways, my desire in writing this book is similar to the purpose of the writer to the Hebrews. I also want to challenge readers to dig deep into God's Word. Like the author of Hebrews, I want to provide a framework based upon a full appreciation of what you and I call the Old Testament (what Jesus simply called the Scriptures). I want you to have confidence about the core teachings of Scripture and how these all hold together within the purposes of God, who is the same yesterday, today, and forever. My hope and prayer is for you to see that one and the same God has been active within and on behalf of his creation from the beginning, and that his way of working in the world is much the same today as it has always been. And in the end, I pray that this book will be an aid in your study as you grow into maturity in your faith in Christ . . . so that one day you too may teach others.

1

God's Timeline

THE FOUNDATION UPON WHICH a Christian theology is constructed is what I call God's Timeline. This is the view that recognizes time, space, and matter—the experience of God's creation—as distinct from God as Creator. Such a distinction also carries with it the idea that all of creation has been made for God's intended purposes and pleasure. Of course, God is perfect in his very nature and in need of nothing outside of himself to satisfy him. Consequently, the cause of God's creative work is his eternal love.

For me to posit that God's Timeline is the very foundation of a Christian theology might at first appear simplistic, but I assure you it is not. In fact, it is this very Timeline that you and I will go back to as our primary reference point for the understanding of everything that we read in Scripture. That's because Scripture, God's Word, is a book written for real people, in real times and places, who live upon a real earth that has a real beginning and end (well, sort of—we'll get to that). All of this has been created by God and for God. He is the one who has established its boundaries and limits, saying, "This far and no farther," in the separation of oceans from the land, the planets in orbit, and in the irreducible complexity of the human cell. In other words, everything belongs to God and he is ultimately in control.

As we seek to reconstruct God's Timeline for his creation, and more specifically for the earth and its inhabitants, we can begin with a fairly simple picture.

Rescue and Renewal

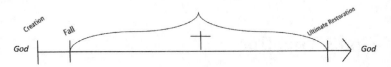

The first thing to notice about this picture is that God and eternity stand outside of the Timeline at both ends. That's because God is eternal and therefore not bound by time. Of course, there is really no way for you and me to wrap our heads around this concept. The picture simply helps us to see that time and space as we know it have a definite beginning point. In other words, there was a "time" (I place this in quotation marks because I am using a human referent to talk about something that defies human description) when the earth did not exist. (Cosmology, i.e., the study of how the earth came into existence, while an important subject that will be touched upon later, is not the focus of this discussion, but simply that God is the one who brought the worlds into existence.)

From the standpoint of eternity, the place of the earth as God's creation looks pretty small and insignificant. In fact, God's creation (including, but not limited to, human beings) has what we call "derived value," i.e., value that comes from God who loves and sustains his creation.

Please understand that this discussion about God's Timeline is not merely philosophical. Rather, this is highly practical and foundational for everything else that will follow in this book. We have to get this part right or else we will have a weak footing right from the start. It's necessary to see that God is distinct from his creation and that creation has a beginning that was established by God for his purpose. Only then can we begin to appreciate the importance of what God has continued to do as he intentionally involves himself in the life of his creation.

Throughout this book, we will be unpacking the various parts of this foundation called God's Timeline. For now, let's proceed with a brief overview of the signposts as marked out in the picture above.

As noted, the earth and all of God's creatures began as an act of God's will and determination. According to the Scriptures, the world was originally designed perfectly without any defects. This subject will be developed further in chapter 2, but for now it's important to recognize that God's original creation reflected his perfect nature. There was no sickness or death, and human beings were given life that had no end (a beginning, yes, but no end). This is the way that God set it up. This was his will and desire for his creation from the beginning.

According to the biblical record, we don't make it very far into human history before we reach the next signpost on the foundational Timeline, namely, the Fall. This is the place where everything and everyone changes. Oh, there still remain marks of God's amazing, original creation. But the Fall introduces something "foreign" to God's original intention for his creation. The Fall brings sin and death.

We will be discussing the Fall in more detail in chapter 3. For now, however, it's important to see how this foundational teaching of Scripture signals a need in the life of God's creation that had not existed until this time. With the disobedience of Adam and Eve, the entire created world became infected with a disease that theologians call "original sin" (given this name because it "originated" with Adam and Eve, not with God, and from which—as human beings are so infected—come forth sinful thoughts, words, and deeds).

It seems that God had created Adam and Eve without sin at the beginning. He also created the rest of the world without susceptibility to disease and destruction. God did, however, create the first humans with the potential for disobedience or sin. (Of course, this whole idea of disobedience leads us to ask about the presence of a law-giver and the concept of justice, subjects that we will touch on later.) At this point it is simply important to note that when sin entered the world, Adam and Eve were not only personally affected, they also affected their DNA that would be passed on to every succeeding person and generation. In addition, their sin resulted in a drastic change for the environment, including plants and animals as well as geologic and atmospheric conditions.

With the Fall, God's creation began to experience many new phenomena that God had never intended. Whereas God had created the world with life, peace, and harmony within all of nature and its various interrelationships, there now existed disharmony, conflict, disease, and death, along with injustice, dishonesty, war, and prejudice (not to mention starvation and an unending stream of natural disasters). In other words, God's world was broken, and it would remain this way unless God chose to intervene and make it right again.

Most of the rest of the Bible is about how God chose to intervene in the life of his creation from the time of the Fall until the Ultimate Restoration. This period, from a human perspective, is long and involved. And the central, foundational point during this period is marked out by the first coming of Christ, which includes the cross and empty tomb. By way of introduction to the Timeline, however, we want to note that this entire period, from Fall to Ultimate Restoration, is what we are calling Rescue and Renewal.

As already mentioned, our Timeline has a cross in the middle of the period called Rescue and Renewal. This is significant as the cross will uniquely shape God's rescue and renewal efforts both prior to and following the first coming of Christ until the final restoration at the second coming of our Lord. (The biblical record leading up to the first coming of Christ is what we usually call the Old Testament, while that period following the first coming is referred to as the New Testament—but more on this later.)

Finally, we reach the point on God's Timeline called Ultimate Restoration. Of course, this designation highlights the fact that the time of Rescue and Renewal does not involve a complete reversal of the Fall for all of God's creation. It will not be until the second coming of Christ when that will be accomplished. (At this point we are using the traditional language of "coming" to talk about Christ, which is more often referred to in the Bible as an "appearing" since God—including the second person of the Holy Trinity—is always present with his creation.)

Before we complete this introductory review of God's Timeline, I would like to point out that the Timeline has an arrow on the end, which indicates an unending existence for God's creation. Whereas the Timeline has a definite beginning, there is no end. Oh, there is an end to the fallen nature of God's creation, a clear and ultimate reversal back to what God originally intended for his creation (only better, since "restored" human beings will no longer have the ability to sin). But there will be no end for God's creation, which continues into eternity.

This Timeline will provide the foundation for every point of doctrine that we will study in Holy Scripture. Every doctrine (or teaching) will fit onto this Timeline and thereby frame (or explain) our understanding. Indeed, every portion of Scripture will become clearer to the extent that we can see where it fits along this Timeline as part of God's plan and purpose for his creation.

Throughout the book I have included several examples of how to apply the Timeline to your study of Scripture so that you can develop a real confidence in how to understand the Bible from a Timeline perspective. The Integrative Questions at the end of each chapter should prove especially helpful in this effort. Now it's time to start building upon our foundation by unpacking the first foundational piece, called Creation.

2

Creation

"IN THE BEGINNING, GOD . . ." This is how the history of the world begins—simply, with God. This world is his creation, thought up in his mind, designed to serve his purposes. Time, as we already noted, is something uniquely constructed by an eternal God for the benefit of his creation. God himself is not bound by the movement of the earth around the sun. We are bound by such things.

Like any great artist, God has placed his imprint on his creation. And he loves it all, not just one part. He made it good . . . "very good" (Genesis 1:31) He fashioned the first man from the dust of the ground and breathed into his nostrils the breath of life, thus making him a living soul. The word for soul in Hebrew refers to the whole person, both the visible and invisible sides of his being. The body itself was ready for life, though incomplete without the life-generating force that comes from God. How fragile and utterly dependent was that first man, and yet he didn't know any differently and was entirely content.

God caused a deep sleep to come upon the man and God took a rib from Adam to make Eve; "Bone of my bone and flesh of my flesh," Adam responded. The two became one flesh in the first marriage, the very institution upon which family, society, and governments would be established.

The first humans walked with God and enjoyed rich and perfect delight within their very beings as well as in every interrelationship upon earth and in heaven. God was certainly present. But then, God is always present with his creation. That was obvious from the beginning, when God spoke the worlds into existence and the Spirit hovered over the face of the waters (Genesis 1:2). Was God beginning to reveal his Trinitarian nature right from the start?

Many have attempted to explain the language that God used to describe human beings as he said that we were made in his image. Genesis puts it this way:

> "Let us make man in our image, after our likeness. And let them have dominion over the fish of the sea and over the birds of the heavens and over the livestock and over all the earth and over every creeping thing that creeps on the earth."

> So God created man in his own image,
> in the image of God he created him;
> male and female he created them.

> And God blessed them. And God said to them, "Be fruitful and multiply and fill the earth and subdue it and have dominion over the fish of the sea and over the birds of the heavens and over every living thing that moves on the earth." And God said, "Behold, I have given you every plant yielding seed that is on the face of all the earth, and every tree with seed in its fruit. You shall have them for food. And to every beast of the earth and to every bird of the heavens and to everything that creeps on the earth, everything that has the breath of life, I have given every green plant for food." And it was so. And God saw everything that he had made, and behold, it was very good. And there was evening and there was morning, the sixth day. (1:26–31)

The most natural way to read or hear anything, no less so the Scriptures, is to take what is said in context. This means that the phrase "image of God" is explained by what immediately follows. As such we hear about God giving human beings dominion over all of creation, including both animals and plants, a sort of co-regency under God (see also 2:15). We also hear the blessing and command to procreate and thereby understand the image of God to be marked by a continuing creation. (It seems important to note that the Hebrew word for "create" as used for God at the beginning of Creation is different from the word for "make," which refers to everything else that is made from the stuff of God's original Creation, like Adam, who was made from the dust of the ground. In other words, we have nothing except that which has been given and provided by the Creator.)

The Hebrew way of making a superlative is to repeat the adjective that describes the noun. In this case God's creation is said to be "good good," or in English, "very good." The God of all creation has left his mark everywhere, especially upon man—"male and female he created them." Everything is full of life and sustenance and purpose. And there is no missing the point that God has put everything in its place.

Another important observation of the Genesis account of Creation comes from the understanding that this book was written within a world that was decidedly polytheistic (many gods). The belief system of such a culture carried the idea that many gods, represented symbolically by earth, sky, rain, animals, and plants, each played a role in providing for the well-being of humankind. It was up to human beings to placate the gods and win their favor, thus insuring the multiplication of crops and children and beasts.

Against this background, the biblical record is unique as it provides a monotheistic (one god) view, with a God who has willingly chosen to provide for his creation without the need to be placated or appeased. This very particular distinction, in fact, would forever shape God's people from this point forward.

A sampling of passages will help to highlight the Bible's accent on the fact that one God brought the worlds into existence for his purposes. For example, when Job questions God's wisdom and judgments, God responds,

> Where were you when I laid the foundation of the earth? Tell me if you have understanding. Who determined its measurements – surely you know! Or who stretched the line upon it? (Job 38:4–5)

Speaking to the greatness of God as Creator and the smallness of man as his creation, the Psalmist asks in amazement,

> When I look at the heavens, the work of your fingers, the moon and the stars, which you have set in place, what is man that you are mindful of him, and the son of man that you care for him? (Psalm 8:3–4)

Even the Apostle Paul, while speaking to Gentiles who had no biblical background, appealed to creation as his starting point for talking about God and his love for all people, saying,

> The God who made the world and everything in it, being Lord of heaven and earth, does not live in temples made of man, nor is he served by human hands, as though he needed anything, since he himself gives to all mankind life and breath and everything. And he made from one man every nation of mankind to live on all the face of the earth, having determined allotted periods and the boundaries of their dwelling places, that they should seek God, in the hope that they might feel their way toward him and find him. Yet he is actually not far from each one of us, for "in him we live and move and have our being . . ." (Acts 17:24-28a)

The most important reason for making such a big deal out of Creation as foundational for our belief system or theology is because the Bible makes such a big deal out of it. An acknowledgement of God as Creator is critical to our understanding of who God is and who we are in our relationship to him and to one another. In addition, it is absolutely necessary to always go back to the beginning of Creation to see God's original handiwork.

Perfection, beauty, harmony, life; all reflect the nature, purpose, desire, and will of the Creator . . . from the beginning. This is important since you and I don't live in the beginning. We've never seen a world like the one originally created by God. We've only heard about it, while fleeting glimpses cause us to long for its return.

Now that we have established that creation was perfect or very good right from the start, complete with boundaries and limits set by God, we are ready to consider the next foundational part of God's Timeline, namely, the Fall.

INTEGRATIVE QUESTIONS:

1. What does the study of creation tell us about the nature of God? Is God one with creation (pantheism)? Is creation simply a part of God (panentheism)? Is God detached from creation (deism)? Is God simultaneously distinct from (transcendent) and intimately involved in and with (imminent) creation?

2. What does a theology of creation tell us about cosmology (the study of the origin of the universe)? If the universe came into existence "accidentally," then what are the implications for our understanding of our purpose and value as human beings?

3. How does the Bible's view of origins affect the following statements?

   A belief in no beginning results in a lack of causality, determination, and purpose.

   A belief in a beginning demands purpose, intelligence, and accountability.

4. How does an originally perfect creation speak against dualism after the Fall? (Dualism teaches that the material world is bad, while the spiritual is good.)

5. Based upon the biblical record, what might be an appropriate view of environmental concerns from the perspective of the Creator?

6. Does the Bible describe one race or multiple races? What is the difference between race and ethnicity? (Hint: the Greek word *ethne* means nation, tribe, or people group.) What are the implications of the answers to these questions for our relationship with those who appear different from us?

7. What is the biblical basis for social institutions such as marriage and family?

8. On what basis might a Christian value the study of science and art? What did the Christian philosopher Arthur Holmes mean by the statement, "All truth is God's truth, wherever it is found," and what are the implications for integrating faith, learning, and life today?

3

The Fall

EVERY MAJOR PHILOSOPHY OR world religion begins with the notion that something is wrong with the world that needs to be fixed. Whether that problem is defined as a faulty perspective or societal ill, every world view begins by positing a problem and then proposing a solution. And Christianity is really no different in this regard.

Christianity recognizes that something has gone terribly wrong with God's creation. As discussed in chapter 2, it is important to understand that creation was originally designed without any problems, but that such a picture of creation is now something that we can only talk about in the past tense.

Ever since the original sin (or Fall) of Adam and Eve, the world has become a different place. Consequently, you and I live in a post-Fall world. We face a world in which we know that our difficulties and hardships, suffering, and death were not part of God's perfect design. And so we have the daily task of trying to live a life in relationship with God and others while aware of the fact that our very lives and those of the people around us are broken and subject to deterioration and eventual death.

One of the things that the Western world, and especially North American Christianity, struggles with is a proper understanding of death. The idea of technological progress, along with death-defying medical and age-escaping cosmetic treatments, has lured us into a prevalent deception that death can be held at bay. And when it comes to actually facing the death of a loved one today, we seem to increasingly remove ourselves from the experience by letting a funeral home take care of everything for a fee, while we show up in time to see a well-preserved body that is quickly set into the ground. Clean, quick, and easy.

Another challenge for the Western world, including North American Christianity, is the way in which everything has become specialized and compartmentalized—especially the human body. If I have a problem with my foot, I need a foot specialist. Of course, if the problem is with a bone in my foot, I will need a bone specialist who works with feet. On the other hand, if the problem in my foot is poor circulation, then I will need to consult a different doctor for that. And so on.

When it comes to the subject of death, we have an even more difficult time understanding the interrelatedness of the whole body. Our tendency is to think of death as simply the absence of vital signs such as a heartbeat or the cessation of breath. From a biblical perspective, however, death is far more pervasive than such a narrow, vital-stats view would suggest.

God told Adam (and apparently, through Adam, Eve) that on the day on which he ate of the fruit from the Tree of the Knowledge of Good and Evil he would surely die. The problem—at least for our compartmentalized Western minds—is that Adam and Eve appear very much alive after having eaten the forbidden fruit. In fact, they go on to live for many years and even have more children. So the question is, what did God mean when he said that the day on which they ate of the fruit they would surely die?

I would suggest that the Bible operates with a much broader and more encompassing view of death than you and I do. Such marks of death can be observed in the responses on the part of Adam and Eve immediately following their disobedience.

We are told that when Adam and Eve ate the fruit, they felt ashamed because they were naked. Up to this point they had not experienced shame and were completely at ease in one another's presence. When the couple heard God in the garden, they ran and hid because they were afraid. Once again, a new feeling was introduced, namely, fear, and this in relation to God. When God asked Adam what had happened, Adam responded by accusing Eve and, indirectly, God ("The woman who *you* gave me"). Finally, as an act of God's judgment, the consequences of the Fall extended to all material properties so that even the ground would not allow food to grow except with great toil, and the relationship between man and animals would be fraught with danger.

It seems that a biblical view of death is much greater than the final cessation of life. Death, from God's point of view, begins with a wide range of symptoms that reflect a break-down and deterioration in every area of life. The very difficulties and hardships that we experience on a daily basis are reflections of the fact that we are at one and the same time both living and dying creatures as a result of the Fall.

I realize this is not a very optimistic view of humanity, whereas God's original creation was made with the perspective of pure optimism. In fact, we desperately want to see ourselves as full of potential, even as we exercise our so-called rights to "life, liberty, and the pursuit of happiness." But the reality is that we do experience shame and fear; we hide from God, ourselves, and others; we easily blame instead of accept responsibility; and eventually our death is complete. Into the ground, mausoleum, or urn we go.

From the time of the Fall, as depicted in Genesis 3, each successive generation reveals the marks of a new human nature from what God originally designed, namely, a sinful human nature. We don't get any farther than the second generation with

Cain and Abel before we witness the first murder in human history, and things only get worse from there. In fact, by the time we reach Genesis 6, God looks upon all of humanity and makes this astounding observation:

> The Lord saw that the wickedness of man was great in the earth, and that every intention of the thoughts of his heart was only evil continually. (6:5)

I don't think this passage gives us any wiggle room when it comes to describing the sinful nature of human beings. The words are absolute. It says that "*every* intention . . . was *only* evil *continually*." Even the very intentions of our thoughts, what prompts our thoughts into existence, are marked out as sinfully motivated. This is a very pessimistic view of human nature. So much for the idea that people are basically good at heart.

Even after the flood, during which Noah and his wife, along with their three sons and wives, were saved, the nature of human beings did not change. As we see from Genesis 8:20–22,

> Then Noah built an altar to the Lord and took some of every clean animal and some of every clean bird and offered burnt offerings on the altar. And when the Lord smelled the pleasing aroma, the Lord said in his heart, "I will never again curse the ground because of man, *for the intention of man's heart is evil from his youth.* Neither will I ever again strike down every living creature as I have done. While the earth remains, seedtime and harvest, cold and heat, summer and winter, day and night, shall not cease. (Emphasis mine)

Once again, it doesn't take long to see the symptoms of the sinful nature in Noah and his three sons, as Noah gets drunk and one of his son's, Ham, shows disrespect toward his father during this incident. And so the effects of the Fall continue with each succeeding generation. In fact, if you follow closely the life of any person in the Bible (for whom enough of their life story has been given), it will not take long before you will be disappointed, whether it's Abraham, Isaac, Jacob, or David.

One of the results of the Fall is that human beings are now utterly corrupted by a sinful nature, with a heart that is completely turned away from God. As David reminds us, this bent is set from the very point of conception:

> Behold, I was brought forth in iniquity, and in sin did my mother conceive me. (Psalm 51:5)

There seems to be no escaping the fact that apart from God's intervention directly within our heart, we would remain forever lost and separated from God. Such will be the topic of the next chapter, on Rescue and Renewal. Before we move ahead too quickly, though, we need to spend a little time discussing what is often referred to as "the problem of evil."

One of the biggest questions that every great philosophy and world religion seeks to address is the question of evil in the world. And, as mentioned earlier, Christianity is no different in this respect. There just seems to be something innate that tells us things are not the way they are supposed to be. When we see natural disasters or injustice, the imbalance of food resources that leads to malnourished children, apartheid, and other forms of prejudice, suffering, and death, we feel a strong and deep sense of (call it primeval) outrage that something has gone terribly wrong.

Christians explain the brokenness of this world by first starting with God's original creation that was free of any defect. The Fall is then given as the explanation for the beginning of sin, suffering, and death in the world. The question, however, that inevitably comes up is this: Where did the serpent come from who tempted Eve (and Adam, "who was with her," Genesis 3:6) to sin?

The presence of Satan in the form of a serpent is itself the introduction of evil within God's perfect world. If God created all things, including Satan, then how can we say that God's world was perfect and without sin? Obviously imperfection did exist, right in the middle of the garden.

In the last book of the Bible, in Revelation 12, we find the clearest description of the origin of evil, namely, Satan. In this highly symbolic vision that was given to John, Satan is described as a dragon that engaged in war to gain heavenly rule over the archangel Michael. In the end, Satan and his angels are thrown down and banished to earth.

> Now war arose in heaven, Michael and his angels fighting against the dragon. And the dragon and his angels fought back, but he was defeated, and there was no longer any place for them in heaven. And the great dragon was thrown down, that ancient serpent, who is called the devil and Satan, the deceiver of the whole world – he was thrown down to the earth, and his angels were thrown down with him. (12:7–9)

The assumption is made that all of God's creation, including the angels, were originally good and without sin or defect. Like Adam and Eve in the garden, however, the angels were created with the ability to distrust and disobey God and thereby fall away from him. So it was with Satan and his angels, which provides the explanation for the origin of evil in the world. As we can see in verse nine above, Satan is known as "the deceiver of the whole world," and his first act of deception on the earth was with Eve.

There is much that we still want to ask about why God set things up the way that he did, especially by giving human beings the ability to turn away from him. This subject will be taken up more fully in a later chapter. For now, however, it may simply be helpful to suggest that the only way God could experience a genuine relationship of love with us, his creatures, is if he gave us the freedom to either continue saying yes to him every day or to reject him.

Since Adam and Eve chose to forfeit the life that God had given them, and the marks of death had already become pervasive, we next need to consider where to find the solution to this problem. And so we turn to the subject of Rescue and Renewal.

INTEGRATIVE QUESTIONS

1. Is the nature of man, following the Fall, basically good or evil? (Are there any marks of God's good creation that remain after the Fall?)

2. Is human progress possible today? Can human nature be regulated (politics, laws)? Can a person be taught not to sin (education)?

3. Does evil exist? On what basis would you say yes? No?

4. What, if anything, does the problem of evil say about the nature of God? (That God isn't all-powerful? That God doesn't care?)

5. What is free will prior to the Fall? After the Fall?

6. How do we diagnose death according to the Scriptures? Consider death under the following categories: mental, emotional, physical, moral.

7. What environmental concerns were introduced as a result of the Fall?

4

Rescue and Renewal

IN THE BEGINNING, GOD . . . . This is how the chapter on Creation began. So too, this is how the present chapter must begin, namely, with God. You see, the Fall was man's turning away from God and forfeiting of the perfect life that God had given. Consequently, the only way for human beings to experience rescue and renewal would be if God intervened on their (our) behalf.

Once again:

> In the beginning, God created the heavens and the earth . . .
> And God said, Let there be light, and there was light . . .
> And God said . . . And God said . . . And God said . . .
> And God said . . . And God said . . . Then God said,
> Let us make man in our image, after our likeness.

This is how Genesis 1 describes the six days of Creation. It's all about God.

Genesis 2 narrows our focus on God's final brushstrokes of his creative work as follows:

> Then the Lord God formed the man of the dust from the ground and breathed into his nostrils the breath of life, and the man became a living creature. And the Lord God planted a garden in Eden, in the east, and there he put the man whom he had formed. And out of the ground the Lord God made to spring up every tree that is pleasant

> to the sight and good for food. The tree of life was in the
> midst of the garden, and the tree of the knowledge of
> good and evil . . . Then the Lord God said, "It is not good
> that the man should be alone; I will make him a helper
> fit for him . . . So the Lord God caused a deep sleep to fall
> upon the man, and while he slept took one of his ribs and
> closed up its place with flesh. And the rib that the Lord
> God had taken from the man he made into a woman and
> brought her to the man. (2:7–22)

It is always important to go back to the original creation
and remember that nothing came into existence unless God
chose for it to be so. We owe our very life and breath to God
our Creator. Likewise, if fallen humanity was to be rescued and
restored it could only happen if God chose to intervene and do
a re-creative work. Fortunately, for you and me and all people,
God loved his creation and chose to intervene.

God came to Adam and Eve, sought them out and found
them. Even though Adam and Eve were running the opposite
direction and trying to hide from God, God did not give up on
them. When God confronted Adam and Eve with their sin and
an opportunity for confession ("Where are you?"), and they
held firm to their conviction that they had done nothing wrong,
God did not abandon them. Finally, God brought the promised
judgment for the consequences of sin upon Adam and Eve, and
condemned Satan who had appeared in the form of a serpent.

Before casting Adam and Eve out of the garden, God did
one more thing. He fashioned garments of animal skin for the
couple to wear and thereby covered their nakedness. Whereas
prior to the Fall they were naked and felt no shame, now their
fallen, sinful nature bore the consequences of sin, which included feelings of discomfort at their nakedness. God, out of
the love for his creation that originated from within his very
nature, covered the couple as an act of restoration. This was a
new thing. Innocent blood was shed to provide such a covering.
But then, this was God's creation. He could do as he pleased.

If we had to select only one passage from Genesis—indeed from all of the Old Testament—that speaks clearly about God's ultimate intentions for his creation, it would have to be Genesis 3:15. This was God's pronouncement of condemnation upon Satan, and God's ultimate promise to correct what had been undone or lost in the Fall. Speaking to Satan (in the form of a serpent), God said,

> I will put enmity between you and the woman, and between your offspring and her offspring; he shall bruise [lit. "strike"] your head, and you shall bruise [lit. "strike"] his heel.

Notice that God makes a dramatic shift from talking about contention between the offspring of Satan and the woman in general to a very singular contest between Satan himself and one of the woman's offspring. It is also instructive to see that the same word, "strike," is used to describe the pain that each one (Satan and the singular "he") will inflict upon the other. The big difference, though, is the position of the heel. While the strike from the serpent on the heel is certainly a deadly one, the crush of the heel upon the serpent's head is an ultimate show of dominance. In other words, even though the woman's offspring ("he") will die in his struggle against Satan, such a death will still bring about the ultimate victory over Satan. This was God's promise.

It's easy for the Christian to see in this passage the death of Christ upon the cross. In fact, theologians usually refer to Genesis 3:15 as the "proto-euangelion" (or "first evangel/gospel"). And while the marks of a promised Savior are certainly clear within this passage, we want to be careful not to read back into it more than the original hearers could have understood. (Fortunately, however, God continued to unfold the revelation of this promise throughout the Old Testament. More on this later.)

One of the beautiful things that is often missed in a reading of Genesis 3 is what comes immediately after God pronounces judgment upon Satan: remarkably, the naming of the woman.

> The man called his wife's name Eve, because she was the mother of all living. (3:20)

Up to this point Adam's wife was simply referred to as "the woman." Now that God had given her the promise of ultimate victory over Satan through her offspring, Adam is making a confession of faith in this promise by naming his wife Eve. The name Eve, in Hebrew, means "living." She will be the one through whom many more generations will come. And she will be the one through whom, ultimately, the Savior of the world will come.

When we fast-forward to Paul in the New Testament, we see how he makes the connection between what God had promised to Eve and its fulfillment in Christ.

> For since death came through a human being, the resurrection of the dead has also come through a human being; for as all die in Adam, so all will be made alive in Christ. But each in his own order: Christ the first fruits, then at his coming those who belong to Christ. Then comes the end, when he hands over the kingdom to God the Father, after he has destroyed every ruler and every authority and power. For he must reign until he has put all his enemies under his feet. The last enemy to be destroyed is death. (1 Corinthians 15:21–26)

Death came through Adam, and the resurrection comes through Jesus Christ. The cross was the venomous death-blow of Satan upon the heel of Jesus, while the resurrection signaled the ultimate victory of Jesus over Satan, sin, and death. And in the final resurrection of "those who belong to Christ," the last enemy, death, will be completely destroyed. The long-awaited offspring of Eve will have come to be the ruler of all those who now live through him. The heel that had been struck has now placed the enemy "under his feet."

Okay, so we know that Jesus has conquered Satan through his death and resurrection. Then why do we still suffer and die? Why hasn't everything been put right, reversed, corrected, and restored? If Christ has risen from the dead, ascended into heaven, and sits at the right hand of God the Father as we confess every week, then why is there still injustice, starvation, natural disasters, genocide, the threat of nuclear war and dirty bombs, the destruction of marriages and families, and the cruelty of deteriorating health and eventual death?

Now for the chapter on the last stage of God's Timeline: the Ultimate Restoration.

INTEGRATIVE QUESTIONS

1. What is the difference in perspectives between Genesis chapters 1 and 2? (Hint: telescoping is when a writer shifts from the general to the specific.)

2. What is the view of human beings and their relationship to God in chapters 1 and 2? Their relationship to one another?

3. Genesis chapter 3 introduces a new character into the biblical record. What, according to Scripture, is the origin of Satan? What is the nature of Satan?

4. How does the popular notion of Self-Help fit with the biblical description of human beings after the Fall? (physically, mentally, emotionally, spiritually)

5. From a comparative religions perspective, why does the idea of a sacrificial substitution (animal or human) seem to have universal appeal?

6. Upon what authority do leaders (religious, philosophical, political, educational, economic) base their claims to have answers to the human dilemma today?

7. Are pain and suffering good? Why? Why not? Scott Peck, in *The Road Less Traveled*, describes pain as a gift. What do you think he means by this?

8. What does C. S. Lewis mean, in *Mere Christianity*, when he says that a personal sense of right and wrong, good and bad, points to the moral law written on our hearts?

5

The Ultimate Restoration

AFTER JESUS HAD RISEN from the dead and before his ascension, he turned to his disciples and said,

> All authority in heaven and on earth has been given to me. Go therefore and make disciples of all nations, baptizing them in the name of the Father and of the Son and of the Holy Spirit, teaching them to observe all that I have commanded you. And behold, I am with you always, to the end of the age. (Matthew 28:18–20)

This is probably the best known among the post-resurrection sayings of Jesus and yet also one of the least understood. Oh, the Christian church has been clear about the need to baptize with the Trinitarian formula. We even have some sense that instruction in the faith needs to follow baptism as an inseparable part of the disciple-making process (although these two, baptism and teaching, have become increasingly divorced from one another, especially in the West). The words spoken by Jesus that I want to focus on in this section, however, are the first and last statements, which bracket the description of how to make disciples: "All authority in heaven and on earth has been given to me . . . And behold, I am with you always, to the end of the age."

According to the words of Jesus, he has placed himself squarely in both heaven and earth at one and the same time.

But our human (especially Western) minds, bound as they are by space and time limits, cannot comprehend what Jesus is saying here. Either he is in heaven or on earth, but not both at the same time. After all, didn't he ascend back to the Father and then send forth the promised Holy Spirit in his place? How could Jesus possibly intend to mean exactly what he says about being with us always (present tense), to the end of the age? And what, by the way, is the end of the age?

In addition to the question of the nature of our Lord's presence here with us, we also have the thorny question of how to understand our Lord's exercise of authority in heaven and on earth. Prior to the ascension, Jesus demonstrated power over wind and waves, demonic entities, physical properties like walking on water and walking through walls, as well as sickness and death. Wherever Jesus went, he corrected what had gone wrong with creation. All of this begs the question, if Jesus is still here, and he has (as he claims) all authority in heaven and on earth, then why don't we see the world being corrected? Where is the great reversal that was supposed to occur with the appearing of Christ?

Many misguided (some downright charlatan) preachers have arisen in every generation with the claim that Jesus is currently reversing (in a final and complete sense) the effects of the Fall today. These so-called teachers of the Bible have a number of Scripture passages that they turn to for support, not the least of which is the one from Matthew 28 above. The problem is that while God does sometimes provide physical healing today, such healing is only temporary. In other words, even when someone is healed today, that person will eventually die. (Of course much investigative work has been done today that has revealed the deceptive practices of many so-called healers.)

Most troubling to me is the fact that so many Christians today don't have a strong enough grasp of God's Word to speak confidently about what God will and will not do between the first and second appearing of Christ. Unfortunately, we have a tendency to either overestimate what God will do today (such as the approach above) or underestimate what God is doing. Most Christians in the Western world, I would suggest, fall into the latter category. Because we don't see the full-blown reversal of God's action in the world, we assume that he isn't doing much of anything (a type of functional atheism if you will).

The most important point of this chapter is to say that God has chosen to undo the effects of this fallen world in three stages. The first stage began when God restored Adam and Eve back into favor with himself and continued up to the first appearing of Christ. The second stage began with the first appearing of Christ and will continue until the second appearing. The third (and final) stage will be ushered in with the second appearing of Christ.

This three-stage understanding of God's work in the world will be described in more detail in later chapters. For now, however, it is important to explain that the first stage in God's rescue and renewal work pertains largely to the nation of Israel in the Old Testament, while the second stage pertains to the church in the New Testament. The third stage is actually the consummation that occurs on the Last Day, when Christ appears, upon which day the reversal will be final and complete and continue through all eternity.

It is the last stage on God's Timeline—the Ultimate Restoration—that occupies our attention in this chapter. This is the Last Day, the Day of the Lord, the Second Coming, the final work of God reversing the effects of the Fall. On this day, everything will be made right. We will be resurrected with bodies that will even surpass that of Adam, bodies that, like the glorified body of the resurrected Lord, cannot be subject to suffering and death. Even the possibility of such will not exist.

On the Last Day, there will be a time of judgment, a separation of those who have a living faith in Christ from those who don't (Matthew 25). There will be a new heaven and new earth, the two brought visibly into alignment in a way not fully

seen before this day (Revelation 21). And there will be a restoration of all of God's creation, back to the way God originally
intended when he first established the world and shared his
presence with Adam and Eve in the garden (Romans 8). Indeed,
at the final resurrection, all of the saints who have preceded
us in death shall be joined with those who still remain. There
will no longer be any sense of separation between these two (1
Thessalonians 4). No wonder John the Revelator ended with the
words, "Amen. Come, Lord Jesus"!

INTEGRATIVE QUESTIONS

1. Is the biblical view of history cyclical, linear, or somehow
    both? Explain.

2. What is the difference between everyday hopes, dreams,
    and expectations and an ultimate hope in God?

3. How much can we/creation be renewed on this side of eter-
    nity?

4. What is meant today by the term "medical necessity"? What
    is the difference between prolonging life and prolonging
    death?

5. In what ways do Christians sometimes talk about heaven
    as a form of escapism? How does the ultimate restoration,
    with a new heaven and earth, affect the way that we view
    our time on earth today?

6. Historically, theologians have referred to our relationship
    with God on this side of eternity as a time of "now, but not
    yet." What is meant by this description?

7. Where, according to the Scriptures, is Jesus right now?

8. What are the three stages/phases of Rescue and Renewal?

6

The Old Covenant People of God

(Stage One of God's Rescue and Renewal)

GOD NOT ONLY CREATED all things, both visible and invisible (as we confess in the Nicene Creed), but, as we have seen in the chapter on Rescue and Renewal, God also creates (and re-creates) a people for himself. The classic covenant language that God uses is to say, "You will be my people, and I will be your God" (Exodus 6:7). Like creation itself, this is all God's doing. He is the one who re-creates, rescues, renews, and, ultimately, restores.

If we, as the New Covenant people of God (post–death and resurrection of Christ, and pre–second appearing), are to understand who we are in our relationship to God, we need to go back and see what it meant to be the people of God *before* the first appearing of Christ. Also, in addition to gaining a better understanding of our relationship to God by looking at the past, we have the opportunity to see how God has remained consistent in who he is and how he has worked (and

continues to work) in the life of his people both pre–first appearing of Christ and post–first appearing of Christ. In other
words, the God of the Old Covenant is the same as that of the
New. (Throughout this book, the word "Testament" is used to
refer to the biblical record, while the word "Covenant" is used
to refer to our promise-based relationship with God as found
in the Scriptures.)

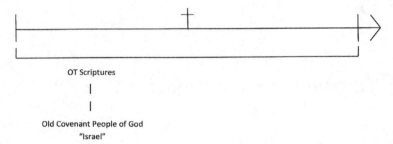

When Christians in the Western part of the world in the
twenty-first century read about the importance of circumcision
and animal sacrifices in the Old Covenant, it sounds strange
to our ears. We have a difficult time understanding how such
practices could ever compare, in their very nature, to the way
that we live out our relationship with the same God today. Part
of the problem in our minds, however, comes from the fact that
we have struggled to accept the very down-to-earth way that
God continues to work in the life of his creation. And another
part of the problem in our minds is that we have grown up
with a misinterpretation of the Old and New Covenants that
has made the Old Covenant Law-based and the New Covenant
grace-based. Let me explain.

First, I want to tackle what seems to be our resistance to
God working in our lives in very physical ways. Somehow it
seems less than "spiritual" for God to attach any real significance to his physical creation when it comes to him establishing
and sustaining a relationship with us. But the truth is, God has

always worked through the material of this world to create and sustain both physical and spiritual life within his people.

When God created Adam, he used the dust of the ground and enlivened him with the breath of life. And Eve was fashioned from the rib of Adam. God sustained the life of Adam and Eve by providing the Tree of Life in the middle of the garden to which he attached the promise that to eat of this tree would result in everlasting life. Of course, there was also a second tree in the garden from which they were forbidden to eat, and doing so resulted in death.

Once the first couple ate of the forbidden fruit and this resulted in death (both spiritual and physical—a rather Greek dichotomy since Hebrew simply calls Adam a "living soul"), God rescued and renewed his relationship with his people (at this point just two, but with the DNA potential for billions). He gave the couple a "covering" of animal skin, a very physical way of demonstrating his love for them, and then gave them the first covenant promise: to one day bring forth an offspring from the woman (a physical, human heir) through whom God would ultimately conquer Satan, sin, and death.

I use the language "covenant promise" in this book as a way to talk about the fact that God establishes a relationship with us (the whole "You will be my people, and I will be your God") as an undeserved promise that began with Adam and Eve. It is this same covenant promise, then, that gets repeated and expanded as we follow the work of God in the lives of his people throughout the Old Testament. (Once again, "Covenant" refers to the relationship that God establishes with his people, whereas "Testament" refers to the segments of Scripture designated as OT—Genesis to Malachi—and NT—Matthew to Revelation.)

After Adam and Eve, we first encounter the covenant promise again with Noah and his family. God had promised to preserve Noah during the flood, after which Noah offered sacrifices from the clean animals that God had directed him to take on board the ark. And God attached his promise to the physical rainbow in the sky that he would never again destroy all flesh through a universal flood. In this way, God would preserve a people for himself just as he had stated implicitly to Eve, and now a little more explicitly to Noah.

The next person in the line of God's covenant promise was the man Abram (his name later changed to Abraham). Abraham was called by God to travel to what would eventually become the land of promise for God's people. And it would be through Abraham and his wife Sarah that God would bring forth a son named Isaac to continue the covenant promise. Of course Isaac became the father of Jacob, whose name was later changed by God to Israel. But we are getting ahead of ourselves. Back to Abraham.

When God gave a more direct and expanded version of his covenant promise to Abraham, he said,

> Go from your country and your kindred and your father's house to the land that I will show you. And I will make of you a great nation, and I will bless you and make your name great, so that you will be a blessing. I will bless those who bless you, and him who dishonors you I will curse, and in you all the families of the earth shall be blessed. (Genesis 12:1–3)

A few chapters later, when God reiterates his covenant promise to Abraham, we hear these important words about Abraham: "And he believed the Lord, and he counted it to him as righteousness" (15:6). Immediately, God reinforced his promise with a vision. He caused a deep sleep to fall upon Abraham (the same language that was used to describe how God caused Adam to fall asleep when God made Eve) and gave him very specific information about how his offspring would be enslaved four hundred years in a foreign land (Egypt) after which they would be established in the land of promise. With this pronouncement God caused a flaming torch to pass between pieces of a heifer that had been cut in half as a way to visually and physically reinforce the covenant promise.

This discussion about God's covenant promise—and the physical ways that he used to establish and reinforce his promises—is foundational when it comes to talking about the fact that the way God worked in the Old Covenant was much the same as he works in the New Covenant. From the Tree of Life to a rainbow and a torch passing through two halves of a heifer, we can see how God has chosen to set apart his creation and attach a promise to it as a way to reinforce his spoken covenant promise. Of course, all of this is in addition to the fact that he continued to unfold the fulfillment of his covenant promise through the very physical gift of offspring, first to Eve and then to Abraham and Sarah.

A popular view of the Bible that has led to much confusion about how God works in the lives of his people centers around the belief that the Old Covenant was based in the Law (or judgment) while the New Covenant is based in the Gospel (or grace). The basic idea is that the Old Covenant people of God were accepted by God based upon their keeping of the Law, while the New Covenant people of God have a relationship with God based upon Jesus' fulfillment of the Law for us, and thus we now live under God's grace apart from works of the Law. Unfortunately, this approach betrays a misunderstanding of both Law and grace, as well as drives a wedge between how God acts in the Old Covenant and the New Covenant.

I think we can already see from the story of Adam and Eve that God is always the one who creates and sustains, then pursues, seeks out, and re-establishes a people for himself. This is the consistent theme that runs throughout all of the Old Testament. And when we get to Abraham, we also hear how it was his faith in God's promises that gave him a righteous standing in his relationship with God. This faith-based relationship with God is the beginning point for all of God's people, not the Law. God's gracious, undeserved favor (seeking out, finding, calling, establishing, gifting with faith and the Holy Spirit) is what makes a people of God possible. It's only upon God's initiative and creation (or re-creation after the Fall) that anyone is brought into a right (righteous) relationship with God, from which follows a life of obedience unto God.

Someone will surely say, "Didn't the people of Israel have to practice circumcision, keep certain feast days like the Passover, and offer animal sacrifices as part of their commitment to God?" The answer is both yes and no. God's Word says that Abraham "believed the Lord, and he counted it to him as righteousness." This belief in the Lord came *before* circumcision or festivals or specially prescribed animal sacrifices. (Even though all three of these practices existed in the ancient Near East among other people groups prior to Abraham, the Lord had not yet prescribed such practices for his people—except for Noah's clean animals for sacrifice—until after he had given Abraham the gift of faith to believe his covenant promise. Remember, at this point there was no person/people named Israel.)

Moses is the next person in the lineage from Adam and Eve, and following Noah and Abraham, to whom God reiterated the covenant promise. Once again it is important to recognize the gracious work of God in establishing for himself a people prior to ever giving the Law.

God called Moses (through a very physical fiery bush) to go and stand before Pharaoh with a message from God, namely, "Let my people go!" In spite of Pharaoh's resistance, God demonstrated his power until Pharaoh commanded Moses and the people to leave. After celebrating the Passover (when God passed over all of the houses of the Israelites where the people had placed the blood of a sacrificial lamb on their doorposts and lintel—a very physical sign as God had instructed), God led his people with a pillar of cloud by day and fire by night (a very specific, located presence of God as distinct from his infinite presence—"The Lord went before them *in* a pillar . . . to lead them," Exodus 13:21) until he led them right up to the shore of the Red Sea. With their backs against the wall of the sea and Pharaoh's army gaining ground in the distance, Moses, speaking on God's behalf, said, "Fear not, stand firm, and see the salvation of the Lord, which he will work for you today. For the Egyptians whom you see today, you shall never see again. The Lord will fight for you, and you have only to be silent" (14:13–14)

Indeed, God chose his people, delivered his people, led his people, and provided for their salvation. Their job was to stand firm, be still, and watch God work on their behalf. Once the Red Sea was parted, all of God's people passed through it, including men, women, and children (with infants and very young children being carried). Of course, the response of the people to God's salvation was to worship with singing and dancing and loud instrumentation. Worship is always the response to God's saving work.

When God had led his people to the foot of Mount Sinai, he called Moses up to himself where God spoke to him out of the mountain, saying,

> Thus you shall say to the house of Jacob, and tell the people of Israel: You yourselves have seen what I did to the Egyptians, and how *I bore you on eagles' wings and brought you to myself.* Now therefore, if you will indeed obey my voice and keep my covenant, you shall be my treasured possession among all peoples, for all the earth is mine; and you shall be to me a kingdom of priests and a holy nation. These are the words that you shall speak to the people of Israel. (Exodus 19:3–6, emphasis mine)

These are the words that God spoke prior to the giving of the Law (the Ten Commandments and their various applications). Once again, God reiterated and expanded the covenant promise to his people. God was victorious over the enemy. God bore his people up and brought them to himself. God re-established a relationship with his people. Only now would he give them the laws that would govern their relationship with him and with one another. But the salvation, mercy, grace, and promise came first.

> Moses came and told the people all the words of the Lord and all the rules. And all the people answered with one voice and said, "All the words that the Lord has spoken we will do." And Moses wrote down all the words of the Lord. He rose early in the morning and built an altar at the foot of the mountain, and twelve pillars, according to the twelve tribes of Israel. And he sent young men of the people of Israel, who offered burnt offerings and sacrificed peace offerings of oxen to the Lord.
>
> And Moses took half of the blood and put it in basins, and half of the blood he threw against the altar. Then he took the Book of the Covenant and read it in the hearing of the people. And they said, "All that the Lord has spoken we will do, and we will be obedient." And Moses took the blood and threw it on the people and said, "Behold the blood of the covenant that the Lord has made with you in accordance with all these words." (Exodus 24:3–8)

The order of God's saving-rescuing-renewing work was always what established the covenant-promise between God and his people throughout the Old Testament. God was the one who took the initiative. God was the one who chose and made a people for himself. Then, *from within* the covenant-promise relationship that God had established, God taught and led his people to live out this new (and renewed) relationship with him.

One of the saddest parts of this story is the fact that, even after all that God had done for his people in delivering them from slavery in Egypt, the first generation did not enter the promised land (except for Joshua and Caleb). The reason for this, as the writer to the Hebrews would explain, was unbelief. While disobedience was certainly a mark of unbelief, the cause of such disobedience was the unbelief itself. The one necessarily follows from the other. (Hebrews 3:12, 16-19) In other words the absence of faith and trust in God's promises (another way of talking about unbelief) was the basis for God's people being cut off from God.

There is one more person that we need to look at to see the reiteration and expansion of the Original Covenant, namely, David. Through the prophet Nathan, God reviewed the history of how he had dwelt specifically and locally among his people (as had been spoken to Moses, that wherever the Lord causes his name to be remembered, there he would make his dwelling—Exodus 20:24; Deuteronomy 12:5). In addition, we hear God reconfirm his covenant promise to David and then extend that promise by saying that he would bring forth a king/kingdom from the offspring of David who would reign for all eternity.

> Now when the king lived in his house and the Lord had given him rest from all his surrounding enemies, the king [David] said to Nathan the prophet, "See now, I dwell in a house of cedar, but the ark of God dwells in a tent." And Nathan said to the king, "Go, do all that is in your heart, for the Lord is with you."

> But that same night the word of the Lord came to Nathan, "Go and tell my servant David, 'Thus says the Lord: Would you build me a house to dwell in? I have not lived in a house since the day I brought up the people of Israel from Egypt to this day, but I have been moving about in a tent for my dwelling. In all places where I have moved with all the people of Israel, did I speak a word with any of the judges of Israel, whom I commanded to shepherd my people Israel, saying, "Why have you not built me a house of cedar?"' Now, therefore, thus you shall say to my servant David, 'Thus says the Lord of hosts, I took you from the pasture, from following the sheep, that you should be prince over my people Israel. And I have been with you wherever you went and have cut off all your enemies from before you . . . When your days are fulfilled and you lie down with your fathers, I will raise up your offspring after you, who shall come from your body, and I will establish his kingdom. He shall build a house for

> my name, and I will establish the throne of his kingdom forever. I will be to him a father, and he shall be to me a son. When he commits iniquity, I will discipline him with the rod of men, with the stripes of the sons of men, but my steadfast love will not depart from him, as I took it from Saul, whom I put away from before you. And your house and your kingdom shall be made sure forever before me. Your throne shall be established forever.'" (2 Samuel 7:1–9, 12–16)

The Old Covenant carries forth an echo of consistency as God unfolds and reconfirms his promises from Adam and Eve to David. God is active in the life of his creation from the beginning, and such involvement has never been interrupted. God would preserve for himself a people, an offspring, a place for his name and dwelling, a son and a king. Blood would be shed, and continue to be shed, from the beginning. God would act and his people would respond. Grace and Word and blood and "amen" would shape the lives of God's people.

The subject of God's foundational grace in both Old and New Covenants will be taken up again in a later chapter. For now, however, we need to explore the substance of faith that shaped the Old Covenant people's relationship with God.

INTEGRATIVE QUESTIONS

1. Most English translations today use the word "Covenant" instead of "Testament" to describe God's promise of forgiveness and new life through the death and resurrection of Jesus. What is the difference between these two words?

2. What is the definition of the Law (in both wide and narrow senses)? What is the definition of the Gospel (in both wide and narrow senses)?

3. Why is Abraham so important to understanding Paul's view of the Gentile's (non-Jew) relationship with God? (See Romans 4 and Galatians 3)

4. The traditional definition of a sacrament is threefold, namely: a) a physical part of God's creation set apart for a special purpose, b) a word of promise attached to that physical part of God's creation, c) instituted by God (or Christ). According to this threefold definition, what were the "sacraments" in the OT?

5. Epistemology is the study of how we acquire knowledge or come to know things. For the Christian it is important to recognize that God reveals himself to us in two ways, namely, through natural or general revelation (God's creation) and through special revelation (God's Word). Can you give a couple of examples of each?

6. Why is it so important that creation, history, and theology not be separated from one another? (Consider the genealogy from Luke 3.)

7. Consider how the study of an automobile may have similarities to the study of Scripture and a relationship with God. For example, we can learn about a car from four different perspectives: pragmatic (usefulness), historical (morphology, physical changes over time), constructive (look/listen under hood), and experiential (drive, feel). Now apply this example to Scripture and a relationship with God.

   Pragmatic:

   Historical:

   Constructive:

   Experiential:

8. Is most of Scripture a list of propositional truths? Or stories (narratives) that teach such truths? Explain?

7

The Prophetic Voice

WHAT DID THE OLD Covenant people of God believe? What was the substance (or content) of their faith? Did they have an assurance following the Fall that God would send a Savior, a Messiah? And if so, how much could they have known about the One who was to come? In other words, if we didn't have the New Testament fulfillment of Jesus to read back into the Old Testament, would there have been enough of God's revelation in the Old Testament to anticipate a promised Savior?

I suppose it could be said in hindsight (looking back from a New Testament, post-first-appearing-of-Christ perspective) that the spoken word of Creation, the Spirit hovering over the waters, and the Tree of Life were all implicitly prophetic in nature, but this would be getting ahead of ourselves. In this chapter, however, we need to begin with the direct, explicit promises that God gave to his people throughout the Old Testament, which formed the substance of their faith in God and his provision of salvation through a Savior.

Our starting place, of course, is the promise to Eve in Genesis 3:15. Since we already covered this in chapter 4, it will be helpful to simply restate that this was the first promise of a Savior who would both suffer and die ("you will strike his heel"), and yet whose death would ultimately conquer Satan, sin, and death ("he will strike your head"). In other words, the one who will strike (or crush) the serpent's head is God's promised Savior.

While it will not be possible in this chapter to provide more than a brief overview of the prophetic (promised offspring of Eve) voice, we do need to see a few of the major examples from the Old Testament to appreciate the substance of the faith that sustained the Old Covenant people of God. In many ways (as we will observe later), everything that happened in the Old Testament pointed ultimately to Christ. Much of this understanding, however, could not be fully understood until the first appearing of Christ, following his death and resurrection. This doesn't mean, though, that the Old Covenant people of God did not have a substantial understanding of God's promise to send a promised Savior.

As we move from the first promise of a Savior to Eve and the preservation of life through Noah, we eventually come to Abraham and the promise that through him all the nations of the world will be blessed. Such was the heart of God for his creation right from the beginning, namely, that all nations/people would be blessed. Here there was no distinction between Jew and Gentile. There was simply "all nations." Consequently, it will help to remember that whatever God did in the life of his people from this point forward, it always included a desire for everyone to know the blessing of God's presence in their lives.

There are many times in the Old Testament when we hear God speak a word of promise that seems to have a partial fulfillment in its immediate historical context and an ultimate fulfillment in the future. The promise to Abraham is such an example as there were multiple, partial fulfillments over time (birth of Isaac, purchase of a burial plot in the land of promise, a nation/"son" brought out of slavery in Egypt to eventually occupy the land of promise, exile and return) until the ultimate fulfillment that would come through the promised offspring of

Eve. Such was also the case with the prophecy given to David about his kingdom.

You will remember 2 Samuel 7:1–9, 12–16 from the previous chapter, in which the statement was made that after David dies God will raise up a son who will build a house for the Lord, and that this son's kingdom will have no end. Notice that there is a twofold promise here: the first that a son will follow David who will build a house for the Lord, and second that this son's kingdom will never end. This is an example of the prophetic voice, which has both an immediate, historical (partial) fulfillment and a later, ultimate (and still very much historical) fulfillment. The first part of the promise was realized in the reign of David's son, Solomon, who built the temple for the Lord, while the second part of the promise, the "whose kingdom will have no end" part, would be fulfilled in the ultimate Son of David who was to come. (David is referred to as "the Anointed One," which in Hebrew is the word *Messiah* and in Greek the word *Christ*. This is where the idea gets carried forward that the ultimate Son of David will be called the Messiah.)

One of the challenges for you and me as readers of the Old Testament is that we hear the prophetic voice as one single prophecy. In the prophecy to David we hear it stated that a son will come forth from David who will build a temple and whose kingdom will have no end. The problem is that when we follow the life of David's son Solomon, we see that he built the temple, but his life also came to an end. In other words, his reign was not eternal. When we adjust for this by considering that the prophet may have been speaking about David's dynasty, and therefore included successive generations of rulers, we still come up short because David's dynasty eventually came to an end. How, then, did the prophet intend for the original hearers to understand the promise to David?

The best way that I have found to explain how this twofold (or, as with Abraham, multifold) fulfillment of prophecy works is to imagine that the prophet is looking at what appears to be one mountain. This one mountain, however, only appears as one because the prophet is looking at it from the front, compressed view. Such a view would look something like this:

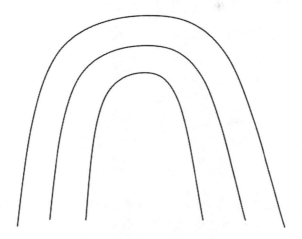

When you look at the prophecy from the side view, however, a very different picture appears. From this perspective you can see multiple mountain ranges with time and space in between, like this:

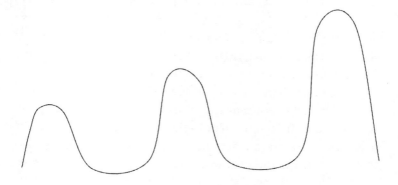

Each mountain range represents a partial fulfillment of the original prophecy. As with our example of the prophecy to

David, we can see a partial fulfillment in Solomon, and then the ultimate fulfillment in the promised Savior:

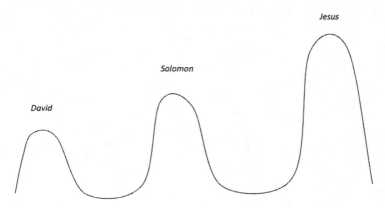

The prophet's front-view perspective is helpful as it explains the tendency among the Old Covenant people of God to collapse the middle fulfillments and focus almost entirely on the ultimate fulfillment part of the prophecy. It seems that while suffering had been foretold for God's Promised Seed/Savior/King/Messiah/Servant/Son, this aspect was sometimes diminished (especially any notion of his death and resurrection). By the first century A.D., such an expectation of immediate victory and dominion over Israel's enemies was so strong that Jesus' own disciples couldn't understand what he was talking about when he explained that he (the Son of Man) would have to suffer, die, and rise again prior to any ultimate fulfillment.

Of course, there are many examples of the prophetic voice in the Old Testament that are so specific and direct that they can only have their fulfillment in the promised Savior. In these instances, there are no partial, multiple-mountain-range fulfillments. Such is the case with Job 19, Isaiah 53, and Daniel 7. (Note, however, that as clear as these following prophesies might appear to us—especially Isaiah 53—the idea of God's Servant suffering to the point of death had often become so minimized/spiritualized that it was practically non-existent in the minds of God's people by the time of the first appearance of Jesus.)

Job probably lived during the time of the patriarchs (Abraham, Isaac, Jacob), even though the book of Job is commonly placed in the section of the Bible known as the Wisdom Books. By the time we reach the middle of Job's story, he has endured the harshest treatment imaginable with the loss of his livelihood, his children, his wife's support, and finally his health. His suffering is beyond comprehension. And then we hear Job speak the following words,

> Oh that my words were written! Oh that they were inscribed in a book! Oh that with an iron pen and lead they were engraved in the rock forever! For I know that my Redeemer lives, and at the last he will stand upon the earth. And after my skin has been destroyed, yet in my flesh I shall see God, whom I shall see for myself, and my eyes shall behold, and not another. (Job 19:24–27)

For our purposes, we want to see that there was a very early expectation of a resurrection from the dead for the people of God, on the Last Day, when a Redeemer, who was also God, would stand (as a man) upon the earth. There is really not a way to talk about any intermediate, partial fulfillment. The prophecy is specific and direct, and can only be seen as fulfilled ultimately in the promised offspring of Eve.

Another great example of the direct application and fulfillment of the prophetic voice comes from Isaiah 53. This is the place where Isaiah receives a very specific word about the promised offspring of Eve, the Servant who will lay down his life for all people and then take his life up again. Whereas earlier passages in Isaiah make reference to a servant with a more immediate application to the children of Israel (described with the inclusive singular as a son or servant), this particular prophecy can only apply to one person. Listen carefully to the way in which the Servant is said to suffer, die, and rise again "for us" (Israel). Also, notice how the Hebrew is written in the past tense, to signal a work on the part of the Suffering Servant that is so sure as to be spoken of as an already-completed action. (I will include bracketed notes throughout the text to highlight the specificity of the promised offspring of Eve, the Suffering Servant.)

Who has believed what he has heard from us? And to whom has the arm of the Lord been revealed? For he grew up before him like a young plant, and like a root out of dry ground; he had no form or majesty that we should look at him, and no beauty that we should desire him [an ordinary man]. He was despised and rejected by men; a man of sorrows, and acquainted with grief; and as one from whom men hide their faces he was despised, and we esteemed him not [not recognized as the one whom God had sent].

Surely he has borne our griefs and carried our sorrows [substitute language]; yet we esteemed him stricken, smitten by God, and afflicted. But he was wounded for our transgressions; he was crushed for our iniquities; upon him was the chastisement that brought us peace, and with his stripes we are healed [substitute, in-our-place language].

And we like sheep have gone astray; we have turned—every one—to his own way; and the Lord has laid on him the iniquity of us all.

He was oppressed, and he was afflicted, yet he opened not his mouth; like a lamb that is led to the slaughter, and like a sheep before its shearers is silent, so he opened not his mouth [self-sacrifice]. By oppression and judgment he was taken away; and as for his generation, who considered that he was cut off out of the land of the living, stricken for the transgressions of my people? And they made his grave with the wicked and with a rich man in his death, although he had done no violence, and there was no deceit in his mouth [an innocent man].

Yet it was the will of the Lord to crush him; he has put him to grief [preordained by God, a necessary "strike of the heel" for the offspring of Eve, God satisfying his own demands through his son]; when his soul makes an offering for guilt, he shall see his offspring; he shall prolong his days; the will of the Lord shall prosper in his hand [after having received the punishment for sin in death, yet will this promised substitute live]. Out of the anguish of his soul he shall see and be satisfied [the best manuscript evidence reads, "shall see the light of life"]; by his knowledge shall the righteous one, my servant, make many to be accounted righteous, and he shall bear their iniquities [because of what this truly righteous one has done, many will be counted righteous on his behalf]. Therefore I will divide him a portion with the many, and he shall divide the spoil with the strong, because he poured out his soul to death and was numbered with the transgressors; yet he bore the sin of many, and makes intercession for the transgressors. (Isaiah 53)

The last, direct prophecy that we will look at in this chapter comes from Daniel 7. This portion of Daniel is the type of literature that we call "apocalyptic," which means that it is highly symbolic in the same way as that of the New Testament book of Revelation. For our purposes here, we want to see how the vision as given to Daniel unfolds both the divine and human natures of the one who was promised from of old, first to Eve (and preserved through Abraham), then to David, and eventually to Isaiah.

DANIEL'S VISION

As I looked, thrones were placed, and the Ancient of Days took his seat; his clothing was white as snow, and the hair of his head like pure wool; his throne was fiery flames; its wheels were burning fire. A stream of fire issued and came out from before him; a thousand thousands served him, and ten thousand times ten thousand stood before him; the court sat in judgment, and the books were opened.

> I looked then because of the sound of the great words that the horn was speaking. And as I looked, the beast was killed, and its body destroyed and given over to be burned with fire. As for the rest of the beasts, their dominion was taken away, but their lives were prolonged for a season and a time.

> I saw in the night visions, and behold, with the clouds of heaven there came one like a son of man, and he came to the Ancient of Days and was presented before him. And to him was given dominion and glory and a kingdom, that all peoples, nations, and languages should serve him; his dominion is an everlasting dominion, which shall not pass away, and his kingdom one that shall not be destroyed. (Daniel 7:9–14)

The Ancient of Days (Hebrew for "Eternal One") who sits upon the throne of judgment is God, and the one who came "like a son of man" and stood before him is both a human and divine figure. He is the one to whom the Ancient of Days gave everlasting "dominion and glory and a kingdom" and before whom "all peoples, nations, and languages should serve."

The picture that we have of the one whom God promised to send, and who would obtain ultimate victory on behalf of God's fallen creation, was revealed over time in multifaceted ways. He would be the promised offspring of Eve, and a descendent of Abraham. He would be the Redeemer who would stand upon the earth on the Last Day and a substitutionary Suffering Servant. He would be the promised Messiah who sits on the throne forever. And finally, he would be the Son of Man who would conquer all dominions and powers in the world as he assumed a unique place of honor in the presence of the Ancient of Days. (Of course, there are many more echoes of this promised one found throughout the Old Testament, and we will look at some of these in the next and later chapters.)

The prophetic voice in the Old Testament gives us the picture of hope that shaped and sustained the faith and life of the people of God throughout this period of God's Timeline.

Beginning with Eve, the people of God shared an expectation that God would eventually send forth one who would correct, reverse, and make right everything that had been undone by the Fall. And so it is to the first appearing of this promised one that we now turn our attention.

INTEGRATIVE QUESTIONS

Note: OT prophets most often spoke for God to address current, contemporary situations, or what theologians call "forth-telling." For our purposes in this chapter, however, we are focusing on the future dimension of the prophet's message, or what is called "fore-telling."

1. When considering the prophet's role of fore-telling, how would you describe the difference between a multistage prophecy and a direct prophecy?

2. Theologians often use the word "type" to describe a person or event in the OT that foreshadows or represents Christ (antitype) in the NT. How does such an observation help us understand the relationship between the OT and NT? What might be some of the dangers of such an approach?

3. During the Intertestamental Period (the 400 years between Malachi and the birth of Christ), many so-called Messiahs claimed to be the fulfillment of OT prophecy. And such a messianic climate is reflected in the writings of the apocryphal books. The problem was that all of these Messiah imposters eventually died, and none of them rose from the dead. How is this messianic fervor similar to what we observe in the "cult of personality" movement today?

4. How does the multistage prophecy from 2 Samuel 7 above reflect the idea of the prophetic "now, but not yet" that we discussed in chapter 5?

5. Based upon the prophecies above, what were the marks or characteristics of the expected Messiah as revealed in the OT?

   Genesis 3:15:

   Job 19:

   2 Samuel 7:

   Isaiah 53:

   Daniel 7:

6. What is the significance of the fact that a large portion of Isaiah 53 was written in the past tense? What was Isaiah's view of Atonement? (See Glossary)

7. How did Jesus answer John the Baptist's disciples when they asked (on behalf of John who was in prison) if Jesus was the promised Messiah? (See Matthew 11:1–6.)

8

Jesus

THE TIME BETWEEN THE Testaments that spans 400 years from Malachi to the birth of Jesus (ca. 4 B.C.) is sometimes called "the silent period." Actually, while the books written during this time (for example, some apocryphal books and non-canonical books from Qumran) have generally been recognized as falling outside of the canon of Scripture, to call this period "silent" is a great misnomer. This was a time filled with reflections and anticipations of God's promised Savior or Messiah (albeit more human than divine). This is also the time during which important work was being done to preserve the Old Testament (from now on OT) in both Hebrew (for example, at Qumran) and Greek (Septuagint). In many ways, this was a time of preparation for the first appearing of Jesus.

The earliest historical documentation that we have about the life of Jesus is found in the four Gospels, namely, Matthew, Mark, Luke, and John (even though Paul's writings actually predate the Gospels). There are some other so-called gospels that have been discovered which date from the middle of the second to the late fourth century A.D. (e.g., the *Gospel of Thomas*). These gospels are not only late in comparison to the canonical Gospels, but they also betray a view of Jesus that is contrary to that of the four Gospels and, consequently, have never been recognized as part of the New Testament (from now on NT). For our purposes, we will focus on the content of the canonical Gospels.

All four of the Gospels provide both shared material and unique material from one another. Matthew, written primarily for a Jewish audience, includes the largest amount of direct OT references. Mark, a shorter work, gives the reader a quick overview (though with some surprising insights along the way). Luke, a historian, wrote with a certain attention to detail and, as such, demonstrates a unique sensitivity to the non-Jewish (or Gentile) audience. And finally there is John, who, writing later than the other three, provides rich supplemental material for the reader. Together, all four of these writers have given us a fuller view of Jesus than one account alone could ever do. As others have said, in the four Gospels we have one story with four angles of sight.

One of the first things that you notice when you begin to read the four Gospels is that the writers assume a deep knowledge of the OT. Who Jesus was, why he came, and what he had to say were all understood from the perspective that Jesus was the fulfillment of the entire OT. Jesus didn't, from the Gospel writer's perspective, just appear out of nowhere. Rather, Jesus was considered to be the continuation and, now, fulfillment of God at work in the life of his people going back to the beginning of creation. In fact, our intention will be to listen carefully to the words of Jesus as recorded in the four Gospels to see how his appearing advances God's Timeline for his creation.

All four Gospel accounts start out with a focus on the "beginning" (or Genesis) of the story of Jesus. Matthew traces the genealogy from Abraham to Jesus. Mark jumps right in with a prophecy from Isaiah about John the Baptist who was sent to prepare the way for Jesus. Luke explains in the greatest detail how God orchestrated the birth of Jesus going all the way back to Adam. And John supplements our understanding of who Jesus is by beginning with his preincarnate existence.

Remarkably, it doesn't take long in the Gospels before we see Jesus appear at the Jordan River to be baptized by John. The significance of this baptism cannot be overstated as it recalls both the beginning of creation and the continuing work of God on behalf of his creation through his Son.

At the beginning of creation, God spoke the worlds into existence. As John tells us in his very first chapter (1:1, 14; compare also John the Baptizer's words, "the one who comes after me was before me"), the Word that God spoke was the second person of the Holy Trinity, namely, Jesus. Of course, this fact was not obvious in the Genesis account. We only learned this later as God revealed his nature throughout the Scriptures. What we do see clearly from the beginning, though, is the presence of the Holy Spirit in the act of Creation. In Genesis 1:2 we're told that the Spirit of God was hovering over the waters. What's interesting for our purposes here is that the Hebrew word used to describe the Spirit as "hovering" is a reference to a bird in flight.

When Jesus came up out of the water, having been baptized by John, the voice of the Father spoke from heaven saying, "This is my son, whom I love. With him I am well pleased" (Matthew 3:17). At that very moment, we're told, the Spirit lighted upon Jesus in the form of a dove. Do you see the connection to Genesis? The Father spoke from heaven about his Son, the Word made flesh, as the Spirit hovered over the waters. In this great event, the Gospel writers reveal their understanding that God is continuing his creative work through his Son, Jesus.

After Jesus was baptized, he was led ("immediately," as Mark records) into a wilderness where he fasted forty days and was tempted/tested by Satan. The very first test, after not eating (and feeling hungry, as the Gospel writers seem compelled to explain), was when Satan said to Jesus, "'If you are the Son of God [i.e., if you are who God said you are at your baptism], command these stones to become loaves of bread.' But he answered, 'It is written, "Man shall not live by bread alone, but by every word that comes from the mouth of God"""" (Matthew 4:3–4).

In the moment of that very first temptation, Jesus signals the beginning of the great reversal. Unlike Adam, who ate from the forbidden tree in the garden, Jesus chooses instead to resist the provocation of Satan and thereby identify himself as the Second (and greater) Adam (a Hebrew word that simply means "man"). Thus the story of Jesus moves from the Creation to the Fall (and its reversal) as a way to signal that God, through this Son of Man, is taking another step in his Timeline to advance the work of Rescue and Renewal on behalf of his creation.

We always want to let Scripture speak for itself and so our approach will be to observe what is actually said about Jesus within the Gospels as we listen to the self-understanding of Jesus in these historical records. As we do this, a number of titles and themes begin to emerge as a way to describe and explain Jesus. Those that we want to consider here are Jesus as Messiah, Son of Man, One Greater than Moses, Son of David, and Son of God.

MESSIAH

The word *Messiah* is a Hebrew word that means "Anointed One." In the Greek NT this word is translated as "Christ." That means whenever you see the word "Christ" in the NT, you can actually read it as "Messiah." This is helpful to keep in mind since the use of the two different words, Messiah and Christ, can give the false impression that we are talking about two different people instead of one and the same person.

As already observed, there was a highly developed expectation from the beginning (Geness 3:15) that God would send forth the seed (usually translated "offspring") of Eve who would ultimately conquer Satan, sin, and death. This promised seed is implicit in the universal blessing to Abraham (through him all the nations of the world will be blessed) and then carried further with the promise to David that his throne would continue eternally. In addition, there were other specific mentions of an Anointed One (Messiah) as found in Isaiah 61:1f and Daniel 9:25, which became even more pronounced during the Intertestamental Period with the apocryphal literature and works from Qumran (representing the late Second Temple Period).

It's helpful to understand the historical development of the expectation of a Messiah so that we can appreciate how prevalent this idea was at the time of Jesus in the first century. We can even see that the idea was embedded in the minds of those outside of Jerusalem as we find, for example, with the Samaritan woman in John 4. After Jesus spoke with the woman at the well and told her personal things about herself that no stranger, let alone a Jew, could possibly know about her, she said,

> "I know that Messiah is coming (he who is called Christ).
> When he comes, he will tell us all things." Jesus said to
> her, "I who speak to you am he." (John 4:25–26)

The Samaritan woman carried an expectation for the Messiah, and Jesus confirmed that he was the fulfillment of that expectation. After this exchange, the woman went back to her town and said to the people,

> "Come, see a man who told me all that I ever did. Can
> this be the Christ?" They went out of the town and were
> coming to him. (4:29–30)

Apparently the people in the town also shared an expectation for a Messiah who would be all-knowing, as they responded by coming out to see Jesus.

Perhaps the most striking instance of Jesus demonstrating his own self-understanding of fulfilling the promise of the Messiah comes from Luke 4. This is the account of Jesus as he taught within the synagogue in Nazareth (an account that, interestingly enough, Luke places immediately following the temptation by Satan in the wilderness).

> And he came to Nazareth, where he had been brought up. And as was his custom, he went to the synagogue on the Sabbath day, and he stood up to read. And the scroll of the prophet Isaiah was given to him. He unrolled the scroll and found the place where it was written,
>
> "The Spirit of the Lord is upon me,
> because he has anointed me
> to proclaim good news to the poor.
> He has sent me to proclaim liberty to the captives
> and recovering of sight to the blind,
> to set at liberty those who are oppressed,
> to proclaim the year of the Lord's favor."
>
> And he rolled up the scroll and gave it back to the attendant and sat down. And the eyes of all in the synagogue were fixed on him. And he began to say to them, "Today this Scripture has been fulfilled in your hearing." (Luke 4:16–21)

As Jesus sat down to teach, he explained the Scriptures in a way that, up to now, had only been experienced as a promise of future fulfillment. Now, in this very moment, the future had arrived in the present, in the person of Jesus. "Today," he said, "this Scripture has been fulfilled in your hearing." From Adam and Eve to Abraham and Moses, to David and the community of Qumran, now the Messiah ("Annointed One") had come. Jesus clearly understood who he was. And what was the initial response of those who were listening to him teach? They simply "marveled at the gracious words that were coming from his mouth." Then they turned to one another and said, "Is not this Joseph's son?" (Luke 4:22). How could such words come from a man (a mere man?) who had grown up right there among them?

SON OF MAN

By far the most common way that Jesus referred to himself during his public ministry was in the third-person with the title Son of Man. And unquestionably, Jesus had in mind the familiar image of Daniel 7 as discussed in the previous chapter. In fact, Luke gives us these words from Jesus about all that will happen at the end of God's Timeline:

> And there will be signs in sun and moon and stars, and on the earth distress of nations in perplexity because of the roaring of the sea and the waves, people fainting with fear and with foreboding of what is coming on the world. For the powers of the heavens will be shaken. And then they will see the Son of Man coming in a cloud with power and great glory. Now when these things begin to take place, straighten up and raise your heads, because your redemption is drawing near. (Luke 21:25–28)

The second to last sentence is an obvious echo of Daniel 7, complete with the Son of Man coming on a cloud. Certainly those who spent time with Jesus made the connection. Eventually, even those who were opposed to Jesus made the connection, which, in part, led to his crucifixion. In other words, our Lord's enemies did not believe what Jesus was saying about himself, but they were very clear about his own self-understanding.

ONE GREATER THAN MOSES

The words "Jesus is greater than Moses" don't actually occur in the NT, although the concept is certainly there, most directly in the Letter to the Hebrews (3:3). The place where I want to go, however, is to the Mount of Transfiguration, especially Luke's account in chapter 9.

Unfortunately, the Mount of Transfiguration is one of the most undervalued stories in the life of Jesus, based simply upon what little ink is devoted to this episode in popular writing today. The fact is, however, that this revelation on the mountain is a critical turning point in the public ministry of Jesus. It was after this event that he "turned his face toward Jerusalem" and made his long descent to Calvary.

This great event on the mountain was an important time of heart preparation for our Lord's disciples (and for you and me as we read the story to the end). This was the place where Jesus pulled back the curtain on heaven and gave three of his disciples an initial glimpse of what had been there all along, namely, the preincarnate glory of the second person of the Holy Trinity, along with all the saints who had preceded the saints on earth.

On this mountaintop Jesus appeared in a cloud (always a sign of God's presence), and alongside of him stood Moses and Elijah (representing the whole OT witness of "Moses and the Prophets"). The three men were in conversation with one another as though they were picking up where they had left off. In other words, these three knew one another well. Each one had been born "in time" with great distances between them, but all three were very much alive and in fellowship together.

As we listen in on the conversation between Jesus and these two glorified saints, we hear (most directly in Luke) the substance of their discussion. They were talking with Jesus about "his departure, which he was about to accomplish at Jerusalem" (9:31). This English translation, however, doesn't let you see the fullness of what was being said. The word translated "departure" is actually the Greek word for "exodus." Do you see how important this is? Jesus is standing there talking to Moses and Elijah about the exodus that Jesus is about to endure. It's as if the three of them are saying, 'Okay, Moses had his exodus, and Elijah had his (chariot of fire). Now it's time for Jesus to complete what God had started so long ago."

Jesus would go to Jerusalem to suffer, die, and rise again, so that in his death and resurrection he could provide the fulfillment of salvation that God had promised to the OT saints. Obviously, Moses and Elijah had been on the receiving end of God's grace long before Jesus appeared in the flesh. Certainly the promise of a Savior to the OT saints had a present power to create and sustain faith long before the death and resurrection of Jesus "in time." Now it was time for Jesus to do "in time" what the promise had already given to those who had believed and trusted in God. Somehow there was an unbreakable connection between the OT covenant promise and the very present reality of Jesus standing alongside of men who, from the perspective of anyone alive at the time (or now as we read this story), had been dead (supposedly) a very long time. Then a cloud came upon all of them, and a voice from the cloud said, "This is my Son, my Chosen One; listen to him!" (Luke 9:35) After they heard this voice, Jesus stood before them alone (the others having vanished) as a way to underscore the fact that Jesus was the ultimate fulfillment of God's promises.

SON OF DAVID

There is no doubt that first-century Judaism had inherited a strong expectation that an Anointed One (i.e., a divinely appointed king) would come forth from David's line to re-establish Israel with Jerusalem as the capital. This Anointed One (in Greek, *Christ*, and in Hebrew, *Messiah*) was expected to overthrow all foreign powers (in this case, the Romans) and usher in a time of unending blessing for the people of God, namely, Israel.

Matthew begins his Gospel account this way: "The book of the genealogy of Jesus Christ, the son of David, the son of Abraham." He then goes on to trace the lineage of Jesus from Abraham, through David, and to the Virgin Mary. (Luke also has a genealogy that begins with Jesus and works back, through David, all the way to Adam.) All of this to say that one of the ways that Jesus came to be known—and remembered—is as the Son of David (see the previous chapter's discussion on 2 Samuel 7).

For the Christian, the beginning of Holy Week is marked out by the celebration of Palm Sunday. This is when Jesus rode into Jerusalem on a colt, the foal of a donkey, and was welcomed by people placing garments and palm branches along the roadway. In addition, the people who were gathered there cried out with loud voices saying, "Hosanna [literally, 'help or save, I pray'] to the Son of David! Blessed is he who comes in the name of the Lord! Hosanna in the highest!" (Matthew 21:9). Mark's account adds the witness of some saying, "Blessed is the coming kingdom of our father David" (Mark 11:10), while Luke relays how some were heard to say, "Blessed is the king" (Luke 19:38), and John includes the words, "Blessed is . . . the king of Israel!" (John 12:13). All of this to say that Jesus was recognized by many gathered in Jerusalem as being the Son of David, the promised king and fulfillment of OT prophecy concerning the Anointed One, or Messiah/Christ, who was to come.

John, writing later than the other Gospel accounts and always good to provide supplemental material, gives the reader important insight as to what was going on in the minds of those who had gathered on that first day of the week. Basically, Jesus was beginning what he knew would be the long week of his passion (or suffering and death), culminating in his resurrection (or glorification). The Pharisees, of course, grew increasingly afraid of Jesus' popularity as they witnessed the large gathering of people hailing him as king (such was also cause for great alarm politically since this could be seen as an insurrection against Roman authority, and the Jewish leaders enjoyed good standing as keepers of the peace). The crowd had been largely motivated by the talk of miracles, especially the raising of Lazarus. But perhaps the most interesting note in John's Gospel is the fact that the disciples themselves didn't truly understand what was happening until after the death and resurrection of Jesus. It would only be after these great events that the disciples would be able to look back and make the connection between what the OT prophets had foretold and what had been unfolding before their very eyes (John 12:16).

SON OF GOD

I have saved the designation Son of God for last because this is by far the most direct way that the Gospel writers identify the unique, divine origin of Jesus as the fulfillment of God's covenant promise to send forth the victorious offspring of Eve. Even with the account of the virgin birth, and the voice of the Father from heaven at the baptism of Jesus and Mount of Transfiguration, the disciples most often lacked confidence in who Jesus really was. But on the night when the disciples were being tossed by wind and waves, and then saw Jesus walk on the water (who enabled Peter to do the same for a brief moment), when Jesus got into the boat and the storm gave way to calm, the disciples responded confidently by bowing down to worship and saying, "Truly you are the Son of God" (Matthew 14:33).

Far and away the most memorable account of the disciples making the connection between Jesus and the God of Israel, however, comes from the confession of Peter.

> When Jesus came into the district of Caesarea Philippi, he asked his disciples, "Who do people say that the Son of Man is?" And they said, "Some say John the Baptist, others say Elijah, and others Jeremiah or one of the prophets." He said to them, "But who do you say that I am?" Simon Peter replied, "You are the Christ, the Son of the living God." And Jesus answered him, "Blessed are you, Simon Bar-Jonah! For flesh and blood has not revealed this to you, but my Father who is in heaven . . ." (Matthew 16:13–17)

Notice that Jesus did not deny what Peter had said, but rather affirmed it as coming directly from the Father. And the language that Peter used is even more striking when we consider that the words "living God" were well known from the writings of Moses (e.g., Deuteronomy 5:26). This link between Jesus and the God who appeared to Moses became—in the very words of Jesus—the confession of faith (or rock) upon which Jesus would build his church. Israel, the OT "church," would continue in the present and beyond, with Jesus, the Son of God, as its foundation. And so, with this in mind, we now turn our attention to the NT church as the continuation, even fulfillment, of the OT people of God.

INTEGRATIVE QUESTIONS

1. Why is it more accurate to talk about the "Gospel" rather than the "Gospels"? (Hint: the Greek text has the heading, "The Gospel According to . . .")

2. What is similar about how all four Gospel accounts begin?

3. The first three Gospel accounts are often called the Synoptic Gospels (prefix syn- = "together," optic = "to see") because they share so much common material and can be read (or "seen") together. What are some of the unique contributions of John's Gospel account?

4. The Intertestamental Period produced a number of Jewish religious groups that appear for the first time in the NT. Can you name them?

5. What were some of the written contributions of the Intertestamental Period? (Hint: Jesus often quotes from one of these.)

6. Theologians often refer to the "analogy of faith" when interpreting Scripture. This means that we let Scripture interpret itself, with the clearer passages taking priority over the less clear passages. When it comes to learning about Jesus, we need to make every effort to let Jesus interpret himself. What was the self-understanding of Jesus as revealed in the four Gospel accounts?

7. What does it mean to make a distinction between us interpreting Scripture and Scripture interpreting us?

9

The Church

(Stage Two of God's Rescue and Renewal)

Jesus understood that he had come "in time" to *continue and fulfill* the forward advancement of God's Timeline. During what is often called the Sermon on the Mount, Jesus taught the following:

> Do not think that I have come to abolish the Law or the Prophets; I have not come to abolish them but to fulfill them. For truly, I say to you, until heaven and earth pass away, not an iota, not a dot, will pass from the Law until all is accomplished. Therefore whoever relaxes one of the least of these commandments and teaches others to do the same will be called least in the kingdom of heaven, but whoever does them and teaches them will be called great in the kingdom of heaven. (Matthew 5:17–19)

In Matthew's account, we have these words recorded that underscore the continuing importance of the Law and the Prophets for those who would trust in Jesus. "The Law and Prophets" is the way in which NT writers summarized the Scriptures (what you and I call the Old Testament) in the first century. In fact, the New Testament can be seen simply as a further explanation and application of the First Scriptures in light of the person and work of Jesus.

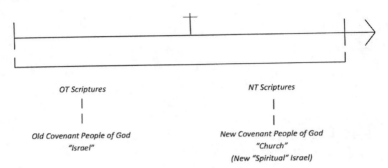

The Day of Pentecost is commonly referred to as the "birthday" of the NT church. This is not a bad designation, but possibly a little misleading as it doesn't take into account the fact that many had come to faith in Jesus prior to this day and also the fact that this day was the fulfillment of prophecy that simply extended God's Timeline through a festival that was already firmly established in the hearts and minds of God's people. On this latter point, it helps to remember that Pentecost was one of the great holy days for Israel, coming fifty days after the feast of Passover. Jesus, of course, was crucified and rose from the dead during the Passover, then forty days later ascended into heaven, after which came Pentecost ten days later. In other words, God continued to act within the framework that he had established with his people long ago.

After the Spirit of God was poured out (not a new thing, as everyone who had faith in God was indwelt by the Spirit, but new in that the focus of the message would now be on the work of Christ accomplished "within time"), the disciples were immediately compelled to go into the streets and begin telling everyone about all that God had done for them in Christ. The disciples spoke in "tongues" (various human languages) as God gave them utterance, and everyone—including, especially, the foreigners—heard about the person and work of Jesus in their own language.

One of the noteworthy things about the message the disciples shared is that it always started with God's Timeline as revealed in the Scriptures (OT) and was now continued and fulfilled in the person of Jesus. Peter's first sermon, for example, makes reference to the prophecy of Joel (Joel 2:28–32) and the Psalms of David (Psalm 16:8–11; 110:1). As mentioned earlier, the disciples finally made the full connection between what had been taught in the Scriptures and what, as Jesus explained, had now been fulfilled right before their very eyes. And the result was that many came to faith in Jesus—as many as three thousand in a single day!

I really can't express strongly enough how what we call the New Testament is simply a reiteration, explanation, application, and continuation of God's Timeline that began with Creation. And this understanding of the NT ought to shape and guide our use of the Scriptures (OT) as a whole in our times of study as well as our preaching and teaching today. (Even Paul, speaking to the non-Jews in Athens, began with Creation and moved quickly to a discussion about Jesus. But more on this later.)

Truly, there is no better model for the importance and practice of teaching the OT Scriptures than Jesus himself. During his initially concealed, post-resurrection appearance on the road to Emmaus, Jesus, seeing how defeated his two travelling companions looked following his crucifixion, said to them,

> "O foolish ones, and slow of heart to believe all that the prophets have spoken! Was it not necessary that the Christ should suffer these things and enter into his glory?" And beginning with Moses and all the Prophets, he interpreted to them in all the Scriptures the things concerning himself. (Luke 24:25–27)

The practice of Jesus and his disciples, both before death and resurrection (Matthew 5:17) and after death and resurrection (Luke 24; Acts 2), was to preach and teach the OT

Scriptures. The gathering of God's people was not intended to be a holy pep talk or motivational speech. Worship was—and still is—a time for looking deeply into the Word of God and learning how God has had mercy on us by allowing us to be included in what he has been doing (and continues to do) according to his will and purpose. Certainly God intends for us to apply the Scriptures to our lives, but even this is to be done within the parameters laid out in the Scriptures.

By far one of the most important texts for understanding God's covenant promise as first given in the OT and then fulfilled in Jesus is found in Jeremiah 31. This is the only place in the OT that speaks directly about a *New* Covenant to come in the future that will supersede the Old Covenant. It's important to note, however, that the Hebrew word used for "new" literally means, "to *renew* or *restore*." In other words, the New Covenant will not be uniquely separate from the Old as though the two didn't have anything in common. Rather, the New will be an extension or fulfillment of the Old. This is critical to understand if we are to appreciate the fact that God's mercy and forgiveness that he provided through the Old Covenant sacrificial system was directly tied to the ultimate suffering and death of Jesus, although in "shadow" form. (This is certainly how the writer to the Hebrews in chapters 8 and 10 understood the fulfillment of Jeremiah 31 in the person and work of Jesus.)

The earliest Christians, as we learn from Paul's writings, understood the New Covenant to have found it's fulfillment in the suffering and death of Jesus. In fact, this was central to the practice of the Lord's Supper in 1 Corinthians 11. Paul, careful to teach the meaning of this sacred meal, reiterates the words of Jesus,

> For I received from the Lord what I also delivered to you, that the Lord Jesus on the night when he was betrayed took bread, and when he had given thanks, he broke it, and said, "This is my body which is for you. Do this in remembrance of me." In the same way also he took the cup, after supper, saying, "This cup is the new covenant

in my blood. Do this, as often as you drink it, in remembrance of me." For as often as you eat this bread and drink the cup, you proclaim the Lord's death until he comes. (11:23–26)

Note that Jesus said the cup is the "new covenant" in his blood. This is the place where God's people would now gather to receive the forgiveness of sins through the blood of the Lord. This was (and is) the place during worship when what Christ accomplished upon the cross was (and is) applied to the lives of God's people, whether the cup was received before the death of Christ (as when first instituted by Jesus with his disciples) or after (as with Paul, along with you and me today). So important was this meal that the first disciples following Pentecost made the Lord's Supper a central part of worship alongside of God's Word, fellowship, and prayer (Acts 2:42).

One of the central themes that I have attempted to underscore up to this point is the inseparable connection and consistency between the faith of Adam and Abraham based upon the Old Covenant promise and the faith of Peter and Paul as taken up in the New Covenant promise. The Old pointed forward "in time" to the first appearing of Christ, while the New points back to the death of Christ as well as forward "until he comes" (1 Corinthians 11:26). This seamless faith connection is what Jesus was talking about when he said to his disciples,

Blessed are your eyes, for they see, and your ears for they hear. For truly, I say to you, many prophets and righteous people longed to see what you see, and did not see it, and to hear what you hear, and did not hear it. (Matthew 13:16–17)

God's Timeline was instituted at Creation and has been carried out, unfolded, progressively revealed, and enacted right on through to the present. From the first shedding of innocent blood to provide a covering for Adam and Eve, to the institution of the Passover with the blood of the lamb during the Exodus, to the sacrificial system at the portable tabernacle/permanent temple, to the suffering and death of Jesus on the cross during Passover, the efficacy of Jesus' death was as certain for Isaiah looking forward (with prophetic past tense, "who was slain") as for you and me as we look back two thousand years today. The same God yesterday, today, and forever was/is at work in and through the second person of the Holy Trinity, namely, Jesus Christ our Lord.

An adequate understanding of the shared faith of Abraham and Paul is necessary as we consider the relationship between OT Israel and the NT church. Jesus selected twelve disciples as a way to underscore the inseparable connection between what he was doing in the first century and what he (the Lord, God) had been doing centuries earlier in the lives of the twelve tribes of Israel (and before them, through Abraham). Of course, this connection becomes all the more clear when we see the twenty-four elders (twelve plus twelve) seated around the throne in heaven (Revelation 4:4), with Judas having been replaced by Matthias (Acts 1:26).

It seems that God has always had a people who were recognized by him as such because of their faith in him and his promises. Even Israel could be subdivided by those who were Israel by birth only and those who were Israel by faith in Yahweh. The prophets of old were very clear about this, and even those non-Jews who joined themselves to Israel and her God (see Ruth) were considered more God's people than those who were Israel by birth only. As Paul explains,

> For not all who are descended from Israel belong to Israel, and not all are children of Abraham because they are his offspring, but "Through Isaac shall your offspring be named." This means that it is not the children of the flesh who are the children of God, but the children of promise are counted as offspring. (Romans 9:6b–8)

Of course, God never counted (or counts) as the people of God those who are only so outwardly by birth or physical marks such as circumcision. Rather, God always (and still) counts as his people those who are like Abraham, who, before the institution of circumcision, believed in God and his promises and, therefore, his faith was counted toward him as righteousness (cf. Genesis 15:1–6 and Romans 4:20–25). Quoting Isaiah 28:16 and Joel 2:32, Paul states,

> For the Scripture says, "Everyone who believes in him will not be put to shame." For there is no distinction between Jew and Greek; for the same Lord is Lord of all, bestowing his riches on all who call on him. For "everyone who calls on the name of the Lord will be saved." (Romans 10:11–13)

It is certainly true that ancient Israel was originally established as the unique people of God. This relationship with God, however, was never intended to exist as the sole possession of Israel until the appearing of Jesus (see Exodus 12:38, "A mixed multitude".) Israel was, in fact, the OT church and, as such, was given the responsibility to be an example for all, even a "Light to the Nations" (Isaiah 42:6 et al.; a title first applied to Israel, and ultimately to Jesus). Unfortunately, Israel became inwardly focused and frequently lost sight of who she was in relation to God as well as her ordained mission to the rest of the world.

Before Jesus ascended back to his Father in heaven, he gave his disciples this command:

> All authority in heaven and on earth has been given to me. Go therefore and make disciples of all nations, baptizing them in the name of the Father and of the Son and of the Holy Spirit, teaching them to observe all that I have commanded you. And behold, I am with you always, to the end of the age. (Matthew 28:18–20)

Jesus, the Word made flesh, through whom the worlds were made, and who voluntarily laid down his life for the sake of all people, gave instructions to his church once again. The message was the same as that which God had given to Abraham, Isaac, and Jacob—namely, "Go to all nations"—and came with the same promise, "I will be with you always." Even the teaching was the same, i.e., God has provided salvation (the name Jesus comes from the Hebrew *Yehoshua*, which means "Yahweh is salvation"). Now, however, circumcision has been replaced by baptism (Colossians 2:11–14) and the teaching has advanced to include the second stage of God's program for renewal in the first appearing of Christ.

I sometimes hear people quote John 1:17—"For the law was given through Moses, grace and truth came through Jesus Christ"—with the suggestion that the OT is somehow void of God's mercy and the NT replaces the commandments found in the OT, instead of seeing that *this passage simply points to the promised Messiah as the hope of God's people both past and present*. Hopefully, by now, the reader can see that the OT is filled with God's grace and truth ("I will be your God and you will be my people"), while the NT builds upon (not replaces) the OT laws and commands of God ("teaching them to observe all things that I have commanded you . . .").

On this latter point, namely, the charge to do all things commanded, we need to remember one of our Lord's last pre–death and resurrection meetings with his disciples recorded in Matthew chapter 25. This is the place where Jesus teaches his disciples (including you and me) in the same manner as the prophets of old. This is the place where Jesus describes the great throne judgment on the Last Day, when Jesus will appear to usher in the last stage of God's Timeline, the ultimate restoration of all things.

The NT church and the OT church have the same basic task. We are to trust Yahweh and his covenant promises and seek to carry out his program of rescue and renewal for all of creation, which includes all nations. This work that God has given us is to be conducted by the power of the same Spirit that was present at the beginning of creation, that created and sustained faith in the lives of Abraham and David, and that now is poured out through the waters of holy baptism today. All of this, of course, is to be done in the strength of the promise that Jesus is with us always to the very end of the age.

Far too often the New Testament is taught and read as though it is superior to the Old (or, as I sometimes prefer, the First) Testament. It almost seems—and, in fact, this is taught by example—that the NT is thought of as a "standalone" document because it contains the record of Jesus' first appearing. Actually, this way of thinking betrays a real and deep misunderstanding of the very nature of God as revealed in all of Scripture. For Yahweh is one God in three persons, and while each person of the one God is distinctly revealed (albeit progressively), where one person is mentioned the other two are present and active as well. In other words, the one God in three persons is inseparable.

It will be helpful to take some time in the next chapter to review the nature of Yahweh as one God in three persons (Holy Trinity) so that we can see how God—who is the same yesterday, today, and forever—has been (and continues to be) at work within his creation.

INTEGRATIVE QUESTIONS

1. Today we sometimes hear sermons in which it is said that "God is doing a new work!" In what way is this statement harmful to a biblical understanding of God? What impression does such a statement leave upon the hearer regarding the relationship between the OT and NT?

2. What is helpful about making a distinction between the *Old* Testament and the *First* Testament?

3. In Genesis 3:15, God gave Adam and Eve the first promise of a Savior. This promise was reiterated and "fleshed out" again with the promise to Abraham, and then again through the prophets. How do you understand the *power* of the promise of God for the OT church when the work of Christ "in time"

was still in the future? How do you explain the promise of the work of Christ "in time" over two thousand years ago as applied to our lives today? (See Romans 1:16–17.)

4. Looking at God's Timeline, how does the fact that God is found outside of the Timeline (beginning and end) help to explain the consistency of God's work within the Timeline?

5. How does the author of the Letter to the Hebrews help us read the OT today? (See especially chapters 8, 9, and 10.) Which laws have been fulfilled with the first appearing of Jesus?

6. How do the teachings of Jesus guide our understanding of how to apply (or not apply) the three types of laws in the OT, namely, the civil, ceremonial, and moral laws? (Hint: The Glossary will be helpful here.)

7. How does a reading of the whole OT (even Leviticus) help us understand our relationship with God today? (Consider the distinction between God's Word "for us" and "to us." See 1 Corinthians 10:6.)

10

The Holy Trinity

You will search in vain to find the word "Trinity" in the Bible. That's because it isn't there. Oh, the concept is in the Bible— which is every bit as strong as a single word—but we have come up with the shorthand word "Trinity" to ease our discussion.

It will be helpful to understand right from the start that Yahweh has revealed himself progressively throughout the Scriptures. What I mean is that God has placed a spotlight on one person of the Trinity more so during one period of his Timeline than another. Oh, the other two persons were definitely present and active, but depending on the one that was being highlighted, the other two were more shadow figures as far as the focal point of attention is concerned.

In the OT we primarily hear about God as One, who frequently revealed himself as a Father (especially toward his son, Israel). That doesn't mean the Son and Spirit were not present, as we will see shortly, but that the Father was the person of the Trinity that God wanted to place the spotlight on more fully (at least during the earlier historical record). When we get to the birth of Jesus the focus shifts dramatically to the life and ministry of the second person of the Trinity (although he constantly points us back to the Father), and then with the ascension of Jesus we find the spotlight placed upon the Spirit (who constantly points us back to the Son, who in turn points us back to the Father).

The earliest hint of there being more than one person at work within the Godhead is found in the very first lines of Genesis:

> In the beginning God created the heavens and the earth. The earth was without form and void, and darkness was over the face of the deep. And the Spirit of God was hovering over the face of the waters. (1:1–2)

God created and the Spirit of God was hovering (a word used to describe a bird in flight) over the face of the waters. The Spirit is spoken of alongside of God at the beginning of creation. (Of course, John would later show that the Son was also present as the Word by which God spoke the world into existence. But we are getting ahead of God's progressive revelation.)

When we continue to the sixth day of creation, we hear God speak these words:

> Then God said, "Let us make man in our image, after our likeness." (1:26a)

What is the meaning of using the pronoun "us" as God references himself? Is this simply, as some commentators suggest, a mere rhetorical device to speak of God's majesty? Or is this another early indication of the triune nature of God that will be more fully articulated as time goes on? I think the latter.

In the OT God was constantly speaking and acting within and on behalf of his creation. He was (and is) neither only immanent (as if to say one and the same with his creation) nor only transcendent (as if to say far away and detached from his creation). He is both distinct from his creation and yet ever present and personally involved. And all three persons of the Trinity get significant play throughout the OT.

Since we have spoken at length about the OT prophetic voice/promise of God's Son who would come into human flesh (chapter seven), I will focus here on the primary way that the second person of the Trinity makes himself known (even flesh-like) in the OT. This has to do with that unique messenger from God commonly referred to as the Angel of the Lord.

The Angel of the Lord (literally, "the Messenger of Yahweh") first makes his appearance in Genesis 16:7–14 when he comforts Hagar after she and Ishmael had been driven away by Sarah. The Angel (the definite article "the" is important here since this is not just any angel) speaks to Hagar as the Lord himself, not on behalf of the Lord—no "thus says the Lord"—as one would expect. And Hagar responds in like manner as though she is addressing God himself (with no correction on the part of the Angel as one would also expect).

Another example of the Angel of the Lord speaking as God himself is when he appeared to Moses in the burning bush. Watch carefully how the Scriptures equate the Angel of the Lord with God:

> And the angel of the Lord appeared to him in a flame of fire out of the midst of a bush. He looked, and behold, the bush was burning, yet it was not consumed. And Moses said, "I will turn aside to see this great sight, why the bush is not burned." When the Lord saw that he turned aside to see, God called to him out of the bush, "Moses, Moses!" And he said, Here I am." Then he said, "Do not come near; take your sandals off your feet, for the place on which you are standing is holy ground." And he said, "I am the God of your father, the God of Abraham, the God of Isaac, and the God of Jacob." And Moses hid his face, for he was afraid to look at God. (Exodus 3:2–6)

Did you see the shift from the Angel of the Lord to God calling Moses from the bush? The two are one and the same; the Angel is God. Why the Angel (or Messenger) of Yahweh? Why not just say Yahweh right from the start? The answer seems to be that God chose to demonstrate his desire to connect with his creation in some intermediary form between divinity and humanity. Indeed, it seems that God was preparing his creation for the advent of his Son in such a way that we could describe

Jesus as "coming into flesh" already in the days of Abraham and Moses.

The Angel of the Lord continues to make appearances to God's people at different times throughout the time leading up to the first appearing of Jesus. Genesis 18 with the three visitors to Abraham is one great example, as is the appearance to Jacob in Genesis 31. Even the obstinate Balaam receives a surprise visit in Numbers 22. In fact, the Angel of the Lord appears some 63 times throughout the Old Testament (see "the angel who has redeemed me" in Genesis 48:16, and such references as found in 2 Samuel 24 and Psalm 34).

The announcement of the birth of Jesus, however, is the point at which a significant language (and content) shift occurs. When Mary received her visitation it was no longer "the" Angel who appeared, but "an" angel that came to her. In Matthew's account (1:20), the definite article has been dropped. While the visit from an angel was certainly significant, this was now only one of an indefinite number of angels—not "the" Angel, as had been the case all along leading up to this climactic point on God's Timeline.

The second person of the Holy Trinity had finally come fully into (human) flesh (in-carnate). The long-awaited Son/Messiah/Savior was conceived by the Holy Spirit within the womb of a virgin. God's plan for his creation had taken a major step forward. The one who previously had been only fully divine before this point would now (willingly) be forever both fully divine and fully human.

Earlier, in chapter 8, we explored in detail the many ways that Jesus revealed himself as the Son of God and the promised Messiah between his birth and ascension. At this point, then, I want to turn our attention to John's Gospel account for the way that he, writing later than the other Gospel writers and thus supplementary and summarily, makes the connection between the Father and the Son in the work of creation as well as Rescue and Renewal.

> In the beginning was the Word, and the Word was with
> God, and the Word was God. He was in the beginning
> with God. All things were made through him, and with-
> out him was not any thing made that was made . . . And
> the Word became flesh and dwelt among us, and we have
> seen his glory, glory as of the only Son from the Father,
> full of grace and truth. (John 1:1–3, 14)

John is crystal clear that Jesus is the Word that spoke the worlds
into existence, and through whom all things were made. There
is simply no missing this point. And when it comes to the
Rescue and Renewal work of God, John recalls for us the very
teachings of Jesus himself on the unique relationship that he
shares with the Father.

The story goes that Jesus was walking in the temple (specifically, Solomon's Colonnade) during the Feast of Dedication
(a time—and place—that would insure a large number of Jews
in attendance), and many worshipers gathered around him and
asked, "How long will you keep us in suspense? If you are the
Christ, tell us plainly" (John 10:24). Jesus, knowing the true
intent of their hearts (seen momentarily in their response),
spoke in a way that would be unmistakable for anyone who was
steeped in the only-one-God belief system (monotheism) of
first-century Judaism and the shepherd imagery of the Scriptures (Psalm 23 comes to mind). Jesus responds to their question this way:

> I told you, and you do not believe. The works that I do in
> my Father's name bear witness about me, but you do not
> believe because you are not part of my flock. My sheep
> hear my voice, and I know them, and they follow me. I
> give them eternal life, and they will never perish, and no
> one will snatch them out of my hand. My Father, who has
> given them to me, is greater than all, and no one is able
> to snatch them out of the Father's hand. I and the Father
> are one. (John 10:25–30)

This response from Jesus could not have been any clearer, which is
obvious from the fact that the original hearers reacted by picking

up rocks to stone him (v. 31). When Jesus asked why they wanted to stone him, they simply stated that it was "for blasphemy, because you, being a man, make yourself God" (v. 33).

For our purposes, we want to see that Jesus had, in one brief exchange, identified himself as a unique person within the one true God. At one and the same time Jesus is both distinct from the Father and yet one with him. The pairing of "No one will snatch them out of my hand" and "No one is able to snatch them out of the Father's hand" is the mark of distinction. And yet also Jesus, in the very same breath, says, "I and the Father are one." Not one person or two gods, but two individual persons, yet one God.

As we move our attention to the third person of the Trinity, namely, the Holy Spirit, it will be helpful to say from the start that there is much misunderstanding today about the nature and work of this divine person. And in my opinion, one of the greatest sources of confusion (at least in popular writings) is a lack of familiarity with the Spirit outside of the New Testament. It seems that because the Spirit of God receives his special highlight during the period following the ascension of Jesus, he is frequently overlooked as having much of a role (together with the Father and the Son) from creation to the first appearing of the Messiah. This is simply not the case, nor should we expect it to be so since where one person of the Holy Trinity is present, likewise also are the other two present (though perhaps more as shadow figures in terms of the primary focus).

We have already noted that God's Spirit was present at the beginning of creation (together with the Father and the Word which later became flesh). But Genesis 1:2 is just the beginning. The Spirit continues to appear significantly throughout God's work within and on behalf of his creation, and especially within his people. In fact, it appears that the Spirit had never left God's people until the time of the flood, when God saw the wickedness of man's heart and said, "My Spirit shall not abide in man forever, for he is flesh; his days shall be 120 years" (Genesis 6:3).

God's Spirit was present and active at the beginning of creation, and this same Spirit continued to sustain the life of God's people thereafter. As human beings turned increasingly away from trust in their Creator and, instead, placed their trust in themselves, God chose to set a period of 120 years prior to the flood, a period during which many could turn back to God for Rescue and Renewal. In the end, however, only eight people would be found upon the ark, and a new beginning (or rescue and renewal of the old) would be established once again.

Job (who probably existed around the time of the patriarchs) is the next place that we turn to hear about the Spirit. Picking up on the work of the Spirit in creation, Job says, "The Spirit of God has made me, and the breath of the Almighty gives me life" (33:4). Obviously the belief in God's Spirit was alive and well early in the biblical record and the hearts of God's people.

The references to God's Spirit in the time leading up to the first appearing of Christ are so numerous that we can only highlight a few for illustrative purposes. Joshua (Numbers 27:18) was recognized as one within whom the Spirit of God dwelt. And David, in the midst of his crisis and confession, cries out, "Take not your Holy Spirit from me!" (Psalm 51:11).

So often I have heard it said that the Spirit of God was not fully given in the Old Testament, and that even those instances where he is mentioned were only for some special gift of leadership. What seems to be missing is an understanding that people prior to the first appearing of Christ were just as dependent on the work of the Spirit in their lives as God's people following the day of Pentecost in Acts 2.

Certainly Joel prophesied that the Spirit of God would be poured out on Israel after going through a severe time of testing (perhaps multiple times of refreshing), a prophecy that was understood by Peter to have been partially fulfilled once again on the day of Pentecost. Joel's prophesy, however, also speaks of the Last Day, the Day of the Lord, when these words will be completely and ultimately fulfilled at the second appearance of

Christ. (Remember the multiple-mountain-range depiction of the prophetic voice from chapter 7.) But there is no hint in Joel's prophecy that the Spirit would be poured out later, on the day of Pentecost, for the first time.

The words of Jesus sometimes throw people off with respect to when the Spirit was poured out into people's lives because, after explaining to his disciples that he would be returning to the Father, Jesus said, "I will ask the Father, and he will give you another Helper, to be with you forever, even the Spirit of truth . . ." (John 14:16–17) Again in that same chapter Jesus says, "These things I have spoken to you while I am still with you. But the Helper, the Holy Spirit, whom the Father will send in my name, he will teach you all things and bring to your remembrance all that I have said to you" (vv. 25–26).

If we just read these verses, then it sounds like the Spirit has not yet come. Of course, that would make about as much sense as saying that the Father was not present with the Son (contrary to Jesus saying, "If you have seem me, then you have seen the Father—the Father and I are one"). What Jesus actually says to his disciples—backing up to John chapter 14 again—is the part that completes verse 17 with respect to the promised Holy Spirit, namely, "You know him [present tense], for he dwells with you [present tense] and will be in you [assurance of a continued presence]." In other words, the promised Holy Spirit was already present, together with the Father and the Son, in and with the people of God, just as he had always been in and with the people of God.

So what's the big deal about Jesus promising the outpouring of the Holy Spirit, and the (partial) fulfillment of Joel's prophecy on the day of Pentecost? It seems that the day of Pentecost signaled a historical fulfillment of God's promise to, more aggressively than before, pour out his Spirit on all flesh, which specifically meant a wide-sweeping work among the Gentiles. This work of the Spirit, along with the fact that the message of the Spirit now included a historical, past-tense reference to the cross and empty tomb, is what was new at Pentecost.

As already noted, we could cite numerous references to the presence and work of the Holy Spirit prior to Pentecost (e.g., Psalm 143:10; 2 Samuel 23:2–3; Isaiah 63:10, just to name a few). The main thing, however, is to note that the three persons of the triune God—Father, Son, and Holy Spirit—have always been together in everything that God has done, which includes the beginning of creation as well as creating and sustaining faith in the heart of God's people, until finally, ultimately, God restores all things (Revelation 21).

Now that we have reviewed the fact that Yahweh in three persons has been active and at work within his creation and his people, we need to look closely at how God has been at work in the life of his people. More specifically, we need to consider God's sacramental presence and the response of God's people in worship.

INTEGRATIVE QUESTIONS

1. Who was the Angel of the Lord in the OT? (See Genesis 48:16.)

2. The Nicene Creed says that Jesus is "of one substance with the Father." How is John's Gospel account helpful as the foundation for this teaching?

3. Review the Apostles' Creed. How is this creed helpful with respect to remembering who God is? What misunderstandings might this creed unintentionally perpetuate about the Holy Spirit? (Hint: consider the length of the section on the Holy Spirit.)

4. The Nicene Creed says that the Holy Spirit "proceeds from the Father and the Son." Does this proceeding only apply to the day of Pentecost and following?

5. While we certainly confess that the Holy Spirit "spoke by the prophets," is there any basis for understanding the Holy Spirit at work in the ordinary believer in the OT?

6. When we call upon the Lord, to whom are we praying?

7. The word "Trinity" is shorthand for a concept that we find taught in the Bible (much like creeds are shorthand). Can you think of any other doctrines for which we use terms that are not found in the Bible (even though the concepts are there)?

11

Worship Before and After the First Appearance of Christ

GOD HAS ALWAYS HAD a people, and he has always had a presence among them. Further, God has always had the practice of setting aside a portion of his creation and attaching a word of promise to that visible, physical creation to reassure his people of his presence (even "located" presence) among them.

We have already observed (chapter 2) how God made a special garden for the first male and female and placed them in it to steward (or manage) it on God's behalf. And yet God was not absent. He "walked with them" in the middle of the garden. Moreover, God set aside part of his creation, namely, two trees (in the very center of their lives), and attached a word of promise to each, one of life and the other of death. Such was the first house of worship, and this of God's design at the beginning of creation.

It is interesting to note that when Adam and Eve were expelled from the garden, they were covered with animal skins that God provided as a part of their restoration. Then, upon their removal from the garden, God placed two angels with flaming swords of fire to stand guard at the gate or entrance to the garden, and this entrance was facing east (a feature that would become increasingly important over time).

Some form of worship (more specifically, man's response to God's loving kindness) continued after Adam and Eve's expulsion from the garden as can be seen in the offerings of Cain and Abel. There was even a growing understanding of how the attitude of the heart was reflected in the manner in which an offering was given as can be observed in the story of this second generation of worshipers.

As we move forward in time to the story of Noah, he is actually directed by God to take additional animals onto the ark for the purpose of offering sacrifices following the flood and the establishment of a renewed creation. In fact, such worship was the first thing that Noah practiced upon stepping down on dry land once again, and this worship was complete with God setting aside a portion of his creation (rainbow) and attaching a word of promise to it.

When we get to Abraham, we see a man who had come out of a background of idol worship that included animal sacrifice, but who now would learn to offer sacrifices in response to God's merciful actions toward him instead of as a means to manipulate the favor of pagan gods. Indeed, Abraham would go on to receive confirmation of God's special presence and promises through the image of God setting aside his creation in the form of a bull (Genesis 15), with his Spirit passing through the two halves of this sacrificial animal.

As we discussed at length earlier, God has always had a people and a special presence among those people. Whether it was the trees in the middle of the garden, the rainbow in the sky, the animals offered in sacrifice, the burning bush, the pillar of cloud by day and fire by night or, eventually, the glory of God in the tabernacle and temple, God, the same yesterday, today, and forever, has acted sacramentally.

The word "sacrament" is from Latin for "mystery." Historically, this word has been used in the church to describe God's action of setting apart a portion of his creation and attaching a word of promise to it. This mystery (or sacrament) carries with it the promise of God's presence to save, forgive, and restore his people. Thus we can see that while the word "sacrament" (in the medieval sense of the term) is not found in the Bible (much like the word "Trinity" is not found), the concept is very real and prevalent throughout the pages of God's Word.

Certainly, the place where the presence of God was made to dwell in a more "permanent" way (I place the word "permanent" in quotes since God's dwelling was/is never bound by creation, although God locates his presence in concrete ways according to his will) was the tabernacle and then the temple. The tabernacle (often called the "tent of meeting") was the portable structure that would be disassembled and reassembled as God led the children of Israel throughout their dessert wanderings, while the temple was the more permanent structure established in Jerusalem during the united monarchy under the rule of David's son, Solomon.

The tabernacle and temple were probably based upon the shrine structures of Egypt (known from archaeology, most notably depicted in the tomb of Tutankhamun) as well as later adaptations from Syria. It would make sense for God to draw upon the practices of the Egyptians when giving directions to Moses for the tabernacle. Egypt is where Moses had grown up and received his education. And what better way for God to demonstrate the redemption of his creation than by taking the best practices on earth (God's earth and creation after all) and using them for his purposes.

Most important for our purposes is the fact that God, more specifically Yahweh, would promise to be present wherever he placed his name. Oh, there is certainly a range of uses for the name of God in the Old Testament, such as the use as an appeal to God's authority (to speak or act "in God's name") or as a mark of possession (for God to place his name upon something or someone). But the truly unique way in which God's name is used is as an equivalent for the very presence and power of God.

Exodus 20:24 is a foundational text for understanding how God's name is used as an exact equivalent for the presence and power of God. Immediately following the giving of the Ten Commandments on Mt. Sinai, we read these words:

> And the Lord said to Moses, "Thus you shall say to the people of Israel: "You have seen for yourselves that I have talked with you from heaven. You shall not make gods of silver to be with me, nor shall you make for yourselves gods of gold. An altar of earth you shall make for me and sacrifice on it your burnt offerings and your peace offerings, your sheep and your oxen. In every place where I cause my name to be remembered I will come to you and bless you."" (Exodus 20:22–24)

Notice that Yahweh is clear about the fact that he is the God of both heaven and earth, and that he shall have no other gods alongside of him. The sacrifices are confirmed because of the fact that this is the place where God causes (his choice) his name to be remembered. Such a remembrance, however, is not just a mere acknowledgement that the sacrifices and worship are for the purpose of recalling what God has done in the past. Rather, the name—which is caused by God himself to be remembered—is the very place (in Hebrew, *makom*) where God says, "I will come to you and bless you." (Again, see Exodus 25:8: "And let them make me a sanctuary, that I may dwell in their midst.")

When Yahweh says to call upon his name in prayer, this is equivalent to calling upon the very presence and power of God. When God commands us not to use his name in vain, he is saying not to dishonor him directly. This *embodied* understanding of God's name helps us to more fully appreciate texts such as Proverbs 18:10, which says, "The name of the Lord is a strong tower; the righteous man runs into it and is safe." And texts such as Joel 2:32 make it clear that to call upon the name of the Lord is to call upon God himself directly.

Yahweh is not bound by his creation. He does, however, condescend (come down, as it were) to reveal himself to human beings in a way that is located in space and time because we, as human beings, *are* bound to God's creation. Over and over again, God has set a portion of his creation aside (the word "holy" means to set apart unto God) to attach a word of promise to it for those who gather for worship. Perhaps even more striking, however, are the ways in which God has actually given his people his unique presence in physical, visible places such as the pillar of cloud by day and fire by night, or as with the tabernacle/temple, the cloud that rested just above the mercy seat in the Holy of Holies (Leviticus 16:2: "I [Yahweh] will appear in the cloud over the mercy seat").

When Solomon built the first permanent temple (or house) *for Yahweh's name* (2 Samuel 7:13), he followed the basic pattern of the portable tabernacle. As for the progression or movement into the courtyard and through the temple, this was much the same as before, from the entrance into the courtyard at the east (an echo of the entrance to the Garden of Eden at the east), complete with laver for ritual washings and the bronze altar for sacrifices (from which, except for whole burnt offerings, the priest and people would commune—"participate together in"—a fellowship meal).

Once the washings and sacrifices were completed, the priest would step up into the first section of the temple, the Holy Place, where he found light provided by lampstands, tables filled with "bread of the Presence," and an altar of incense at which he would offer up prayers on behalf of himself and all of the people. A veil separated the Holy Place from the Most Holy Place (in Hebrew, literally, "Holy of Holies") in which stood the Ark of the Covenant, the winged creatures (remember the entrance to Eden after the Fall?), and the cloud of God's presence. Only the high priest could enter the Most Holy Place, and this only once a year on the Day of Atonement, when special offerings were made on behalf of all of the people and blood was placed upon the mercy seat (the top cover of the Ark), i.e., the place of God's located presence in the midst of his people.

The question often comes up, "What happened to the presence of God after the destruction of the temple and during the period of exile?" The answer is that God had always promised to be present wherever his Word was remembered, whether spoken and read or attached to a portion of God's creation (tree, rainbow, cloud, blood). Consequently, the Word spoken, read, and remembered became central in the lives of God's people during the time of exile, with the hope and expectation that God's located presence above the mercy seat would one day be restored.

Following the second temple, which had been built under Ezra and Nehemiah after the return from Babylon, there arose what is commonly referred to as the religion of Judaism. With this group, an expansion of the temple was begun in Jerusalem by Herod in about 20–19 B.C. This is the temple that Jesus frequented, first as an infant and again at age twelve, and then with his cleansing of the moneychangers. And this is the temple that was destroyed—as Jesus had predicted—by the Romans in A.D. 70. But perhaps most importantly, this is the temple that the Jewish leaders thought Jesus was referring to when he uttered the famous words, "Destroy this temple, and in three days I will raise it up" (John 2:19). Of course Jesus was speaking of his human body and, in so doing, helps us to understand that God's presence in the tabernacle and temple(s) was a foreshadowing of what would be fulfilled in the person of God's Son, Jesus.

Once we have studied the tabernacle and temple, it's easy to see how the major elements of worship find their ultimate expression in Jesus. The writer to the Hebrews is especially keen to point this out. But Jesus himself had much to say on this subject, for example when he calls himself the light of the world (lampstands) or bread of life (bread of the Presence). And certainly the sacrificial system found its termination with the perfect sacrifice of the Messiah upon the cross. But the question still remains, "Did Jesus provide for his people following his ascension anything like the located presence that he gave to his people under the Old Covenant?"

Yes, Jesus did indeed give his people the promise of his located presence here on earth during the period between his ascension and final appearing on the Last Day. And such is not really too hard to imagine once we see that God is the same yesterday, today, and forever, and continues to maintain an active presence in the life of his creation while he fills all things both in heaven and on earth. Just like the people of God who came before the first appearing of the Messiah, those who followed were/are no less in need of physical assurances. As before, God sets apart portions of his creation and attaches a word of promise to them so that we—who are weak and in constant need of reassurance—can know where God may be found.

Whereas the temple had its laver for ritual washings (literally "sea," which calls to mind the beginning of creation and the Red Sea), so too Jesus has instituted baptism. And along with the fellowship meal (literally "communion" or "participation") that came from the sacrifices upon the altar, so now Jesus has given us his body and blood in the Lord's Supper. Of course, all of this is connected to the Word of promise as instituted by the Lord himself. And now, instead of a mere man going into the Most Holy Place on our behalf, Jesus has become our high priest who, as both fully human and fully divine, gives us entry to the throne of grace whenever we call upon his name.

Some people today seem to have a hard time accepting the idea that God would continue to come to us in physical ways. And yet, God has always worked in the lives of his people through physical means. Certainly this is most humbling to our minds, especially in the West, where we tend to think of God's physical workings as somehow "primitive" and beneath what we need today. Until our Lord appears on the Last Day, however, there seems to be a need for us to receive God's Word and the promise of his presence attached to his visible, physical creation.

The two physical ways that Jesus instituted whereby we experience his located presence today are baptism and the Lord's Supper. These two are more than mere signs (although they are that too). These are the places—like the cloud that led Moses in the dessert and then rested above the mercy seat in the Most Holy Place—where God gives us the assurance that more is going on than mere water, bread, and wine.

BAPTISM

When the Jewish leader Nicodemus came to Jesus to learn more about his teachings, Jesus said to him,

> Truly, truly, I say to you, unless one is born again he cannot see the kingdom of God. (John 3:3)

Because Nicodemus was puzzled by this idea of being born again (also translated as "regeneration" or "rebirth"), Jesus went on to explain more specifically how such a rebirth was to happen,

> Truly, truly, I say to you, unless one is born of water and the Spirit, he cannot enter the kingdom of God. (3:5)

These words of Jesus are found, in context, following the baptism of John, who, speaking of the difference between his baptism and the baptism that Jesus would institute, said,

> . . . he who sent me to baptize with water said to me, "He on whom you see the Spirit descend and remain, this is he who baptizes with the Holy Spirit." (1:33)

Unlike John's baptism, which was only mere water and was given as an outward sign of an inward work, the baptism that Jesus instituted would actually deliver the Holy Spirit. Mere water? Yes. But when set apart by God with a word of promise, this mere water becomes a physical, visible, located presence of God's Spirit.

Paul understood the connection that Jesus had made between the water, Spirit, and word as can be seen in his Letter to Titus, where he says,

> But when the goodness and loving kindness of God our Savior appeared, he saved us, not because of works done by us in righteousness, but according to his own mercy, by the washing of regeneration and renewal of the Holy Spirit, whom he poured out on us richly through Jesus Christ our Savior, so that being justified by his grace we might become heirs according to the hope of eternal life. (Titus 3:4–7)

How are we saved? According to God's mercy in Christ and not because of our own efforts. By what means does God apply his mercy to our lives? By the washing (water) of regeneration (rebirth, born again) and renewal of the Holy Spirit, whom God poured out on us (water imagery again). And what does such baptizing do? Paul, again, is our guide:

> Do you not know that all of us who have been baptized into Christ Jesus were baptized into his death? We were buried therefore with him by baptism into death, in order that, just as Christ was raised from the dead by the glory of the Father, we too might walk in newness of life. (Romans 6:3–4)

Paul explains that something very important actually happens when we are baptized, namely, we are connected, united to the very death and resurrection of Christ. In other words, the merits of Christ and all that he accomplished are applied to our lives as though we had died on the cross and risen from the dead. We have been united with Christ through baptism and now have, by the power of the Holy Spirit, begun to live a new life by that same Spirit. (See Paul again in Galatians 3:27, where he says that in baptism we have "put on Christ.") Wow, so much for baptism being a mere symbolic act of obedience!

Whether it was Peter preaching on the day of Pentecost ("Repent and be baptized . . . for the forgiveness of your sins, and you will receive the gift of the Holy Spirit," Acts 2:38), or Peter's explanation in his first letter ("Baptism . . . now saves you," 1 Peter 3:21), or Paul again explaining that baptism is the new circumcision (Colossians 2:11–12), it is clear that the apostles understood the importance of what Jesus had taught them. Consequently, the question that a person of faith needs to ask isn't "How can such a thing be possible?" but rather, "How can I learn to trust what our Lord has given us?" For it was Jesus who, following his resurrection and prior to his ascension, turned to his disciples and said,

> All authority in heaven and on earth has been given to me. Go therefore and make disciples of all nations, baptizing them in the name of the Father and of the Son and of the Holy Spirit, teaching them to observe all that I commanded you. And behold, I am with you always, to the end of the age. (Matthew 28:18–20)

Christ is ruler over all things, both in heaven and on earth. He is the one who sends us to make disciples (believers, the born-again ones). And how does he do this? Through baptizing in God's name ("Wherever I place my name, there I will be present," Exodus 20:24; also see Aaron's threefold blessing in Numbers 6:22–27) and teaching the Word. And what is the promise? That Jesus is with us always. But isn't he about to ascend into heaven? Yes, but he is not bound by heaven. Such is an expression of authority (heaven and earth) not limited location. He is still here!

LORD'S SUPPER

Eucharist, Communion, Table Fellowship, Second Sacrament, Last Supper—all are terms that have been used to discuss what Jesus did on the night in which he was betrayed. In the simplest terms, Jesus took bread and gave it to his disciples, "saying, 'This is my body, which is given for you. Do this in remembrance of me.' And likewise the cup after they had eaten, saying, 'This cup that is poured out for you is the new covenant in my blood'" (Luke 22:19–20). Such seemingly simple words, yet how great has been the debate throughout the years.

Actually, any serious debates about the nature of the Lord's Supper (my choice of term as a way to keep straight whose supper this is) didn't really occur during the first four centuries of the church (with the notable exception of Ignatius, which we will look at later). The church simply accepted the words as instituted by Jesus and reiterated by Paul until the 1500s with the period known as the Reformation, and even then most of the church only questioned the degree of Christ's presence in the meal.

Today, most of Christendom (a way of talking about all believers in Christ everywhere) accepts and practices that Christ is truly present in the Lord's Supper. And with the current move among many churches to "get back" to the first-century understanding of church, we see more and more openness among people to suspend what they have been taught and simply ask of the Scriptures, "What have we been given?" Which brings us back to the writings of Paul, especially to the church in Corinth, and the church fathers who wrote during the first few centuries following the ascension of Christ.

Most writers tend to start with a discussion of Paul on the Lord's Supper by turning to 1 Corinthians 11. To really understand Paul, however, we need to begin with chapter 10. This is where he talks about the fact that Christ was present with the Israelites during their wilderness wanderings, and was even responsible for the water that flowed out of the rock. Somehow, we are told, the Israelites received both physical water and spiritual drink because the rock that followed them was Christ himself. Unfortunately, the Israelites did not appreciate that God was present in this physical provision and so they turned their hearts away from him.

This discussion about Christ being present with the rock in the wilderness forms the backdrop of what Paul then goes on to teach about what the people of God at Corinth receive in the Lord's Supper. He says,

> The cup of blessing that we bless, is it not a participation in the blood of Christ? The bread that we break, is it not a participation in the body of Christ? (1 Corinthians 10:16)

These questions, in Greek, require an affirmative answer, namely, "Of course it is [a participation in the blood . . . body]." And as for our understanding of the word "participation" (Greek, *koinonia*), the grammar makes it clear that the focus is on the blood and body and not on some form of fellowship in this meal. In other words, Paul is saying, "This is a partaking of the blood . . . body" (a real, albeit mysterious, connection to the person of Christ, not unlike that which occurs in baptism).

Of course, all of this talk of partaking in the body and blood of Christ is very strange to our Western ears. We become rather queasy at the idea of what sounds to us like a cannibalistic practice. Our internal reflex automatically resists this as far too physical. Such, however, is what we have made out of this meal. If we simply stick with the words that Paul received and passed on to us, then we don't need to get caught up in a philosophical discussion about the "degree" or "mode" of Christ's presence. Rather, we can simply say in faith that this is what we have been given.

I mentioned earlier that Ignatius was the one exception during the first few centuries of the church where we find a defense of the Lord's Supper. When confronting the Docetics (a Gnostic group that held that all things physical are evil, while only the spirit is good—such a view led them to teach that Jesus was only divine and not human) on the question of the Lord's Supper (or Eucharist), he said,

They [the Docetics] abstain from the Eucharist and
prayer because they do not admit that the Eucharist is
the flesh of our savior Jesus Christ, which suffered for
our sins, which the Father in his goodness raised up. (Ignatius, *To the Smyrnaeans* 6)

Interestingly, Ignatius saw that a denial of the physical, human
nature of Christ led directly to a degradation of the Eucharist.
This is because the early church fathers simply accepted the
fact that Christ, who is both fully human and fully divine, was
physically/humanly present in this meal.

I find it remarkable that some Christians want to raise the
spoken Word of God to a higher level, while relegating baptism to a lower place of importance and the Lord's Supper even
lower still. It looks like the old Docetic/Gnostic dichotomy that
Ignatius contended against whereby somehow the "audible"
Word was considered more spiritual than the visible, physical
Word in the sacraments. Of course, the spoken Word is never
separated from the Word made flesh (as if Christ could be divided). Remember, God has always had a way of taking a part
of his physical creation, setting it apart, and attaching a word of
promise to it. And God has actually given us his located presence in physical places so that we, his people, can have the assurance of his presence through all of the senses, i.e., hearing,
sight, sound, smell, feel, and taste.

Much has been written about the mode of Christ's presence in the Lord's Supper. The pendulum has been swung to
both extremes, with one side saying there is only bread and
wine and the other that there is only body and blood. But the
words as given simply say that Jesus took the bread and cup and
said, "'Take, eat; this is my body. . . . Drink of it, all of you, for
this is my blood'" (Matthew 26:26, 27). And why has this meal
been given? Jesus tells us himself, namely, "for the forgiveness
of sins" (v. 28). Bread? Yes. Body? Yes. Wine? Yes. Blood? Yes.
For the forgiveness of sins? Yes. Can we explain it any further?
No! (Explaining how this works would be analogous to saying

that we can explain baptism, or the two natures of Christ—faith simply responds by saying, "Thank you, Lord, for what you have given me.")

The Lord's Supper is also important as it pertains to God's Timeline because this celebration (Eucharist means "thanksgiving") marks our time between the first and second appearing of Christ. Or, as Paul explains,

> For as often as you eat this bread and drink the cup, you proclaim the Lord's death until he comes. (1 Corinthians 11:26)

INTEGRATIVE QUESTIONS

1. Theologians often use the Latin term *extra nos* (literally, "outside of ourselves") to describe the *origin* of the gift of faith that God gives us to believe his promises. Why is this understanding of faith important?

2. Saving faith is different from ordinary faith (i.e., belief based upon experience) because saving faith clings to that which it cannot fully see. How does your reading of 1 Corinthians 2:12–14 help you to understand the nature of saving faith?

3. Saving faith has been described as being like a hand that clings to the promises of God. As we see in 1 Corinthians 2 above, the Holy Spirit creates and sustains the gift of faith, which actually "accepts" the truths of God's Word. How does such an understanding of faith lead us to talk about the basis or cause of our salvation?

4. What is the threefold biblical definition of a sacrament? What are some examples of sacraments in the OT? What are the sacraments in the NT?

5. How did the OT sacraments *foreshadow* those instituted by Christ in the NT?

6. What does it mean when theologians describe the NT sacraments as "means" or "instruments" of grace?

7. Theologians often make a distinction between sacramental acts and sacrificial acts of worship. Can you explain the difference between these two types of actions? Does one necessarily come before the other and, if so, why?

8. How are all three persons of the Trinity involved in the sacraments?

Conclusion

GOD'S TIMELINE IS GOD'S Timeline. Simple, but profound. He designed it. He set it up. And he is ultimately in charge of it (which includes you and me and all people) to the very end. Keeping all of this in mind, then, I hope that you have been able to see how God is the same yesterday, today, and forever, especially when it comes to how God works in the lives of his people throughout all of Scripture. I also hope that you have been able to see the Trinity in sharper relief, as all three persons have been (and continue to be) involved in every aspect of God's Creation, Rescue and Renewal, and Ultimate Restoration work on behalf of his creation. In addition, it has also been my desire that you would grow in your appreciation of God's love for the physical nature of his creation and the many ways that he has always been present and at work in and through his physical, visible creation.

God's Timeline is so much more than a way of picturing the course of God's creation (although it certainly is that too). This picture is the very foundation and framework upon which everything else has been, and continues to be, built. God started it, maintains it, intervenes to rescue and renew it, and, ultimately, will restore it. The only reason we know this is because God has chosen to reveal it to us. We could be left to wonder about the past and future of this created world and our place in it. But God, in his infinite wisdom, has pulled back the curtain on eternity to give us a glimpse of what he has been up to all along. We can either choose to ignore God's revelation, or we can dive in and learn everything possible about who God is and what he is doing.

Personally, I have chosen to dive into God's Word and learn what I can during the time that I have been given. Oh, I expect to continue learning throughout all of eternity. But for now, I have a job to do. I need to learn so that I can pass on to others what God has given us. I would suggest that you need to do the same. Hopefully, with this book you have been given a foundation and framework upon which you can construct a clearer understanding of God's Word. It is my fervent prayer that as you read, study, pray and learn, that you will be able to see how each part of God's Word fits into a coherent whole along the path of God's Timeline. And may you grow in your confidence as you eagerly share the treasure of God's Word with others.

Glossary of Terms

(for Deeper Comprehension)

Abraham

Abram (later named Abraham), married to Sarai (later named Sarah), called by Yahweh to go to Canaan (the land of promise) and through whom God promised that all nations of the world would be blessed. Abraham was first in the line of the patriarchs followed by Isaac and Jacob. He also believed God and this gift of faith was counted to him as righteousness. Such a faith, the Apostle Paul says, is the basis for true righteousness for all who believe in Yahweh's promises, especially that of a Savior.

Age

A word used in the OT and NT as a reference to the Last Days (or New Covenant Era), which began with the first appearance of Christ and will conclude with the second appearance of Christ.

Analogy of Faith

A phrase used to describe the practice of allowing Scripture to interpret itself. Such is the case when a seemingly unclear passage is interpreted in light of those passages that are clear and consistent with one another.

Angels and Demons

Spirit beings that were created prior to human beings and that served the purposes of Yahweh. When the angel Lucifer rebelled he took one third of the angels with him, and these became known as fallen angels or demons. (Revelation 12:3–4, 7–9)

Apocrypha

A group of writings composed during the four hundred years between Malachi and Matthew (see Intertestamental Period). These writings reflect the faith of many Jews in the post–Second Temple Era, and include a strong messianic expectation.

Apostles' Creed

A statement of faith from the fourth century A.D. that assembled portions of Scripture to underscore the Trinitarian nature of God, with a special emphasis on the person and work of Christ.

Appearing of Christ

The word "appearing" is used most frequently in the NT to describe what is often called the "coming" of Christ. To "appear" has the advantage of recognizing that Christ is always present, just not to the naked eye, whereas to "come" suggests more of a spatial limitation on the presence of Christ. It is important, however, to appreciate the fact that the language of second coming carries with it a sense of visibility and finality and thus should be retained where used in Scripture.

Ascension

The visible, bodily ascent of the post-resurrected Christ, the account of which is found at the end of Luke and the beginning of Acts.

Atheism

The belief (or "worldview") that there is no such thing as a plurality of gods or a single God.

Atonement

The English word "at-one-ment" is used to translate a word that means to substitute an innocent life for a guilty one, and thus to remove the barrier of guilt between two people or between God and man. Such a substitution means that the two are now at-one with each other.

Baptism

NT sacrament, instituted by Christ, in which God's promises of forgiveness and new life are attached to water and administered in the name of the triune God.

Blood of the Covenant

A phrase used in both the OT and NT to describe how God ratified (put into effect) his promise to rescue and renew a fallen people for himself. The blood is the central, physical element of atonement.

Canon

A word used in biblical studies that means "rule" or "measure" and refers to the sixty-six books included in the Bible. These books are said to be canonical (rule and norm for faith) because of their recognized use within Judaism and the church.

Ceremonial Laws

Laws instituted by Yahweh at Mt. Sinai as found in Exodus, expanded upon in Leviticus and Numbers, and reiterated in Deuteronomy. These laws were specific to the formation of the nation Israel to regulate its worship practices. They were especially designed to emphasize the holiness of God and the need for sinners to be made acceptable to God by his gracious provision.

Church

This English term translates a NT word that literally means "called-out ones" and is used to describe a local congregation or gathering of Christians, as well as the collective, universal church.

Civil Laws

Laws instituted by Yahweh at Mt. Sinai as found in Exodus, expanded upon in Leviticus and Numbers, and reiterated in Deuteronomy. These laws were specific to the formation of the nation Israel to regulate its daily life. They were especially designed to emphasize the fact that God's people were to be unique among other nations in their faithfulness to the one true God, and to teach how to carry out the second table of the Ten Commandments regarding one's neighbor.

Commandments

These are the "imperatives" that God gives to reveal his holy nature and to direct the lives of his people. One of the first examples of God's commands is when he told Adam not to eat from the Tree of the Knowledge of Good and Evil.

Comparative Religions

The study of world religions that emphasizes the similarities between religions, with minimal attention given to the distinct differences.

Content of Faith

The substance or object of one's faith. Theologians distinguish (albeit artificially) between the subjective act of believing and the object of belief. An example of the object would be Yahweh and his promises.

Cosmology

The study of the origins of the universe. Modern approaches tend to leave out the spiritual dimension of creation and thereby support a naturalistic view, whereas the Bible teaches *ex nihilo*, that God created the world "out of nothing" by the power of his Word. (See also Dualism.)

Covenant

This is the English translation of a word that means "promise" or "agreement." The word "covenant" is often found alongside of the word "to cut" in the Hebrew OT, and is usually translated into English as "made" (i.e., Yahweh made a covenant). To "cut a covenant" refers to the act of cutting an animal in sacrifice and thus carries forth the necessity of shedding blood.

Creation (theology of)

This is the study of God and how he brought the worlds into existence by his will and for his purposes. The biblical view of creation teaches that in the beginning God made his creation "very good" and therefore without sin and death.

Creed

From the Latin *credo*, which means "I believe." A creed is simply a statement of belief, or the externalization and articulation of a worldview. For one to claim that he does not believe in anything is itself a statement of belief, namely, that one cannot know if anything is true or real. Consequently, everyone has a creed.

Death

Theologically death is the result of Adam and Eve's sin (see Original Sin). Biblically, death is a term that can be understood in a narrow and wide sense. The narrow sense of death refers to the ultimate cessation of life, while the wide sense includes multiple, interrelated facets of life such as a breakdown physically, mentally, emotionally, relationally, spiritually, all of which eventually end in the narrow sense of death. Medically, it is often helpful to distinguish between prolonging life and prolonging death.

Deism

Historically, deism is a relatively modern idea that posits that God set the world in motion (or wound it up like a clock), then stepped away and let it run on its own without any intervention.

Derived Value

Philosophically, this term carries forth the idea that all of creation, especially human beings, has value that is not self-assigned but rather given (or derived) by the Creator.

Design

The notion that creation reflects purpose in its irreducible complexity on the molecular level has led to the twentieth-century belief that design demands an intelligent source. Not everyone who accepts design, however, believes in a Creator or God.

Determinism

Christian philosophers make a distinction between hard determinism and soft determinism. Hard determinism says that people do not act voluntarily but only as God prescribes (this removes human responsibility). Soft determinism, on the other hand, says that people act voluntarily according to their will and desire (nature), while God is still ultimately in control (this keeps human responsibility and purpose intact, while also recognizing God's sovereign control).

Docetism

This word comes from a Greek term which means "to seem" and is associated with a schismatic group that grew within the Christian church during the fourth and fifth centuries A.D. and taught a Gnostic dualism that Jesus appeared (or seemed) to be human yet was only spirit. This same idea about Jesus is taught in Islam as found in the Quran, Sura 4:157–58.

Doctrine

This English term translates one of the words for "teaching," which usually denotes a primary, codified belief such as the virgin birth or resurrection of Christ. (This is to be distinguished from the word "doctrinaire," which refers to an attitude of condescension.)

Dualism

A belief that creation is made up of two parts (even worlds), namely, matter and spirit, and that the material is intrinsically evil while the spiritual is good. The ultimate goal for a dualist is to eventually escape the material world to experience the goodness and freedom of the spiritual world.

Environmentalism

At the most basic level, an environmentalist believes that nature or creation is intrinsically good and necessary for life. From this perspective one seeks to protect and preserve the viability of creation.

Epistemology

From the Greek word *episteme*, which means "knowledge," epistemology is the study of whether or not truth exists and how one may acquire it. In theology a distinction is made between Natural Revelation (what can be known from the study of creation) and Special Revelation (what can only be known through Scripture). (See both terms.)

Escapism

This term carries forth the idea that the ultimate goal of human beings is to escape the material world for the spiritual. Some Christians have this belief based upon a dualistic view of the world. (See Dualism.)

Eschatology

From the Greek word *eschaton*, which means "last things." In theology the word "eschatology" refers to the study of what will happen between the first and second coming of Christ (sometimes called the last days), as well as what can be expected on the Last Day or Ultimate Restoration.

Eternity

Theologically, this is a term that seeks to describe the fact that God has no beginning or end. He simply is (or in human categories was, is and forever will be). The soul of each person, while it has a definite beginning, is designed to have no end.

Ethics

This is the study of how one ought to live in relation to self, others, and all of creation. Such a discipline presupposes the notion (relative or not) that there exists an internally or communally constructed system of right and wrong.

Evil

Such is the belief that categories of good and bad, right and wrong truly exist within this world, and that some actions or events are bad enough to warrant their description as evil. (See Original Sin.)

Extra Nos

A Latin term that means "outside of us," and used by theologians to describe the fact that salvation is something that comes to us from outside of ourselves. (See also Content [or Object] of Faith.)

Faith

In modern use, faith can be a way of talking about a belief based upon study or experience. While not unrelated, the use of this term biblically and theologically denotes two main uses, either the object/content of one's faith (that which is believed) or the act of believing itself. Such belief (including both objective and subjective elements) describes the spiritual gift of faith, otherwise referred to by theologians as "saving faith." (Again see Content [or Object] of Faith.)

Fall

The second, primary stage on God's Timeline, which describes the action and result of Adam and Eve's disobedience ("falling away") in relation to God.

Father

While the word itself is not common for the first person of the Trinity, this is a frequent, conceptual reference to Yahweh in the OT in relation to collective Israel as his son. In the NT, Jesus frequently refers to God as his Father, even teaching his disciples to pray, "Our Father."

Forgiveness

The English translation of several different words that literally mean "to cover" (Psalm 32:1), "to remove," even "to expunge" (Psalm 103:12), and "to wash away" (Psalm 51:3). The first meaning carries the idea of placing a garment over someone so as not to see his/her nakedness, while the second and following meanings speak of a debt that has been completely erased.

Free Will

A term used by theologians to describe volition, decision making, or choice on the part of human beings and their actions. The concept of freedom is used to describe actions in two realms, namely, the civil and spiritual realms. After the Fall, human beings are said to have civil freedom but not spiritual freedom since they are fallen and unable to respond with hearts of gratitude toward God apart from God's intervention. (See Extra Nos.)

Fulfillment

A biblical term used to describe when God's promises come to fruition within time and space. Such would be the first appearing of Christ as foretold in the OT, as well as the second appearing as foretold in both the OT and NT.

General (or Natural) Revelation

A category of epistemology used to reference the fact that much can be learned about the Creator/Designer, Yahweh, by simply studying creation. This category is distinguished from Special Revelation, which refers to God's revelation of knowledge and truth through his Son, Jesus, and the Scriptures.

Gentiles

A term used in the NT to reference all non-Jewish people.

God

A general, biblical term, often found preceded by the personal name for God, namely, Yahweh, and translated together in English as "Lord God."

Gospel

The biblical term *evangel* literally means "good news" and comes from the ancient practice of a herald running on foot to announce victory in battle over an enemy. Such was applied to the person and work of Christ in his victory over Satan, sin, and death. Theologically the word "gospel" is used in both a wide and a narrow sense. In a wide-sense the word refers to the entire life and ministry of Christ, whereas the narrow-sense refers to the forgiveness (hence, good news) that we have in Christ.

Grace

A biblical term that refers to the action of God toward fallen human beings as he chooses to forgive them all of their sins when such is not deserved. This concept is prevalent throughout both the OT and NT. Students of the Bible have often used the word as an acronym that stands for God's Riches At Christ's Expense.

Healing

A biblical term that has both a wide- and narrow-sense meaning. The wide sense applies to the temporal, human experience of wholeness, whether physical, mental, emotional, spiritual or relational, while the narrow sense pertains to the Ultimate Restoration at the second appearing of Christ on the Last Day.

History

A philosophical term that references time in the past, often divided up into periods for the sake of noting changes or differences in human dispersion, culture, technology, and practice.

Biblically, theologians identify all of history in relation to God as Creator and Sustainer, as well as the one who brings all things to an ultimate conclusion for his purposes. As such, while history may have many repetitive cycles, it necessarily remains linear and purposeful.

Holy Spirit

The third person of the Trinity, present at the beginning of creation, "hovering [like a bird in flight] over the waters." The Holy Spirit (often just Spirit) is distinguished from the spirit (or soul) of human beings in English by a capital S, and is the person of the Trinity by whom human beings are united with God.

Hope

A biblical term that can have both a wide- and narrow-sense meaning. The wide-sense applies to general, temporal hopes (lower case h) such as the hope for good health or gainful employment. Narrow-sense Hope (capital H), however, refers to that which is anticipated on the Last Day with the Ultimate Restoration of God's creation, especially for those who have saving faith in Christ. (See also Faith.)

Human Nature

Biblically, theologians note that the constitution (original design and function) of human beings was perfect, i.e., without sin or susceptibility to decay and death. With the Fall, the very nature of human beings was changed to include sin, thus necessitating God's intervention to Rescue and Renew his creation through his Son, Jesus. Philosophically and theologically, human nature equates with anthropology (*anthropos* = man, *logos* = the word about or study of).

Image of God

This term comes from the pronouncement of God who said, "Let us make man in our own image, after our own likeness" (Genesis 1:26). The exact nature of this image is then described by characteristics such as dominion over creation as caretakers, and fruitfulness as co-creators. In addition, God endowed human beings with reason or rational thought by which to comprehend categories such as good and evil, right and wrong, as well as love and hate (what philosophers call "ethics").

Immanent

A philosophical (though biblically consistent) term that is often used of God to describe his deeply personal involvement with his creation. (Compare with Transcendent.)

Interpretation

A term that carries forth the idea of putting into our own words what the Scriptures teach. Such can be majesterial (what we decide), or ministerial (what Scripture decides). (See Analogy of Faith.)

Intertestamental Period

The period between the testaments, namely, the four hundred years from Malachi to the birth of Christ during which no OT prophets spoke (thus, often called the Silent Period). Increasingly, students of the Bible see this period as an important time of preparation during which much important writing occurred such as the Apocrypha, Septuagint, and Scrolls of Qumran (or Dead Sea Scrolls).

Israel

The name given by Yahweh to Jacob after Jacob wrestled with God. The name means "God strives or holds on tight." The name

Israel became the designation of God's people who entered the promised land of Canaan. In the NT the Apostle Paul uses the term to designate all who trust in Yahweh like Abraham did (i.e., "spiritual Israel"). Today the name is associated with a place and ethnic people.

Jews

The name associated with adherents of Judaism, which is a religious system that came into existence during the Intertestamental Period. Jews are also recognized as those who resettled the region of Israel during the Second Temple Period.

Last Day(s)

As a plural form, this term is used in both OT and NT to designate the time following the birth of Christ until the Last Day (singular), when Jesus will appear on earth for the Ultimate Restoration.

Law

A word that translates the Hebrew *torah* and can be used in a wide or narrow sense. In the wide sense, Law refers to all of God's Word (especially the first five books of the OT, the Books of Moses), whereas the narrow sense refers to the statutes or commands of God. (Theologically we say that the narrow sense of Law Shows Our Sins, while the narrow sense of the Gospel Shows Our Savior, or S.O.S.)

Located Presence

A term used by theologians to distinguish the unique, special presence of God from the nature of God as omnipresent (i.e., present everywhere). Such a distinction becomes important when talking about the "sacramental" presence of God in both OT and NT.

Lord

The English word used to translate the personal name for God, namely, Yahweh, as distinguished from the more general term for God. (The title LORD is capitalized in the English Bible to distinguish it from any other god, or even a man depending on the context.)

Lord's Supper

The special, sacramental meal as described by the Apostle Paul (1 Corinthians 11), who passed along that which he had received as instituted by our Lord Jesus Christ (Matthew 26, Mark 14, Luke 22) "on the night when he was betrayed."

Material

The physical, visible world as we know it. Strict materialists believe that such physical properties are all that exist, while a biblical view holds to God's creation as including both that which is visible and invisible. (See Nicene Creed.)

Means of Grace

Theological term used to reference any physical property to which God attaches a word of promise to remember, save, and protect his people. Also called Instruments or Channels of Grace. (See Baptism and Lord's Supper.)

Mercy

A biblical word meaning "to feel loving kindness toward another," often used to describe the heart of God toward his creation, especially human beings. This word, in reference to God, underscores his personal nature as including compassion. From this starting point within the "heart" of God, he then demonstrates mercy by giving grace (or gifts). (See John 3:16.)

Messiah

A biblical term used to translate the Hebrew OT word for "anointed one," and is often a reference to a king, especially the long-promised Son of David who will sit on his father's throne forever. The Greek NT translates this word as *Christ*.

Monotheism

A belief held by Judaism, Christianity, and Islam that there is only one God, as opposed to polytheism, which teaches that there are many gods. The latter view was dominant among contemporary belief systems within the biblical world.

Moral Laws

A theological category of law distinguished from the Ceremonial and Civil Laws given to Moses at Mt. Sinai. These latter laws had temporary value as they applied to the nation of Israel in Canaan. The former laws—the Moral Laws—were codified in the Ten Commandments and simply clarified that which had been written on the hearts of all human beings.

Narrative Truth

A term used to describe the ordinary way that God reveals himself in the Bible, in distinction from Propositional Truth, which systematically lists categories of beliefs. The Bible conveys truth through the stories of real people and events at real times and places. Such underscores the historical nature of God at work in and through his creation.

New Heaven and New Earth

A somewhat veiled OT promise (although see Isaiah 65–66), yet a clearly revealed NT promise, that on the Last Day when Jesus appears a second time he will usher in the Ultimate Restoration of his creation. This ultimate New Creation describes the reversal of the effects of sin and a fallen world so as to bring about a New Earth that is joined to Heaven, never to be separated.

New Life

A biblical term used to describe the presence and activity of the Holy Spirit within a human being. The Holy Spirit creates and sustains saving faith, which clings to the promises of God, and thereby makes the unwilling heart willing to love and trust God. In the OT this New Life was based on a faith in the promised Messiah to come, while the NT faith is based upon the Messiah who has come and will come again.

Nicene Creed

Fourth-century creedal statement adopted at the Council of Constantinople (A.D. 381) for the purpose of clarifying the nature of God as Creator of all things (visible and invisible) and to state against Arius that the Father and Son are of the same substance and, thus, both fully one God. (Arius had taught that Jesus was divine, but created or made like all of God's creation. Hence, the language "begotten" was used to describe the relationship of the Son to the Father.)

Now, Not Yet

This phrase captures the tension that exists between the first and second coming of Christ. While Christ has come to usher in his reign through the Word and sacraments, such activity is more internal (Now), though certainly with outward effects, whereas the ultimate restoration will not occur until the Last Day, when Christ appears once again (Not Yet).

Original Sin

Theologians use this term to reference the new state of being that existed within Adam and Eve as a result of their first disobedience. Their disobedience, or Fall, has been passed on to each succeeding generation as a sinful nature. From this broken, fallen nature, then, spring forth all sinful thoughts, words, and deeds.

Panentheism

Unlike Pantheism, which means that "everything is God," Panentheism means that somehow "everything is part of God" (or *en*, "in" God), but not the total sum of God. This fine distinction, while unbiblical, allows those who hold this belief to still see God as bigger than all material things.

Pantheism

This is the belief that "all is God." There is no distinction between everything material or spiritual and God. In this view, we are God.

People of God

Another term for Sons of God or Children of God, this title refers to those who are on the receiving end of God's grace and recipients of Saving faith. This title comes from God's promise, namely, "I will be your God, and you will be my people."

Pharisee

A small but dominant group of religious leaders within Judaism during the time of Jesus, the Pharisees taught strict adherence to the Torah (the Law, or first five books of the Bible, also called the Books of Moses) and physical separation from the Gentiles.

Philosophy

This word, literally "love of wisdom," is a general term that applies to the in- depth study of any subject. In the study of theology and religion, philosophy refers to the questions/study of life in relation to God and others, and may or may not include ideas directly addressed by Scripture, e.g., the study of etymology (the origin and development of certain words).

Presence of Christ

This term carries forward the idea that Christ, while truly present everywhere at the same time (omnipresent), has also made himself present in particular, located ways. Such a unique presence is called the sacramental presence of Christ.

Progress

When applied to the philosophy or study of being, this term suggests that humans evolve from lesser stages to higher forms. Such a perspective on human origins and technology is rather elitist as it doesn't account for the technological contributions at every level, nor the fact that human beings have not changed fundamentally since the beginning.

Progressive Revelation

When applied to the study of revelation, this word indicates the gradual way in which God has unfolded his plan of salvation (or Timeline) from Genesis to Revelation.

Promised Seed

Seed, often translated as offspring, appears for the first time in Genesis 3:15. This is the promise given to Eve that one from among her offspring would ultimately conquer Satan (the originator of sin and death). This promised seed motif is seen again in the promise to Abraham and his seed, and finally realized in the offspring of Mary, namely, Jesus.

Prophecy

A term that translates a range of meanings that can only be determined by its context. Prophecy most often refers to the role of the prophet as a forth-teller, i.e., one who speaks God's Word for an immediate situation. Less often (though a more popular notion) is the use of the term for the act of fore-telling, or speaking of something that will occur in the future. As to this last use, it is helpful to distinguish between multiple and direct fulfillment. Multiple fulfillment is when a prophecy has multiple, partial fulfillments leading to its ultimate fulfillment in Christ, whereas a direct fulfillment has only one fulfillment in Christ.

Propositional Truth

When a belief, doctrine or teaching is stated in a formulaic and concise manner (systematically), this is called a propositional truth claim. While the Bible does have a number of formulaic and direct confessional statements, most of its teachings are found embedded within the stories or narratives of Scripture.

Qumran

This is the place name of an ancient town located on the northwest corner of the Dead Sea where several caves were discovered in 1947 and which contained thousands of scroll fragments (hence the name Dead Sea Scrolls), many of which have been reassembled and found to be copies of books of the OT. The scrolls and Jewish community have been dated to around the second century B.C. and include many non-biblical writings that reflect a strong expectation for a Messiah.

Rebirth

This term is often used to translate a Greek NT word that is also translated into English as regeneration, and is found first on the lips of Jesus in his explanation to Nicodemus on how to enter the kingdom of God, namely, by being reborn of both water and the Spirit. This same word is used by the Apostle Paul in Titus 3 in relation to baptism.

Redeemer

A word that means "to purchase or buy back," redeem is used in the Bible to describe God's action of rescuing and renewing his wayward people as his own possession. This concept is ultimately applied to the person and work of Christ, who gave his life as the full payment for the sins of all people, and as such he is called the Redeemer.

Remembrance

A term that, when used by God, has both a past and present force. In other words, when God says to remember one of his saving acts (e.g., the rainbow calls to mind salvation from the flood), this remembrance has the force of God continuing to carry out his promises in the present. The word "remember" is often connected to God's name, which is another way of talking about God's presence. (Exodus 20:22–24; 1 Corinthians 11:24–25.)

Rescue and Renewal

This language designates the period that spans the Fall of Genesis 3 until the Ultimate Restoration on the Last Day when Christ returns/appears upon the earth. This period of Rescue and Renewal can be divided into three stages, namely: 1) pre–birth of Christ, 2) earthly ministry of Christ, and 3) post–ascension of Christ.

Resurrection

The belief in a general resurrection from the dead at the end of time, or Last Day, is reflected early in the biblical record (Job 19:25–27). This would be a time of physical restoration. Among the Jews in the NT the Sadducees were unique in that their belief system did not include a general resurrection.

Reversal

This word is used to describe the action of God turning back the results of sin on behalf of his creation. A partial reversal can be observed prior to the Last Day and usually focuses on the internal change of heart and life by the Spirit, with certain visible, physical signs such as the care of those in need by God's people. When Jesus performed miracles of healing, these underscored the fact that God cares for the whole person as well as pointed back to God's original will for his creation. A full and complete reversal will occur at the time of the Ultimate Restoration on the Last Day.

Sacrament

From the Latin Vulgate, sacramentum means "mystery" and is based upon the text of 1 Corinthians 4:1. During the Middle Ages this word became used as a shorthand, technical term to refer to baptism and the Lord's Supper. The concept of sacrament has been used in a general way to describe the manner in which God has worked in the lives of people from the beginning by setting aside a portion of his creation and attaching a word of promise to that creation.

Sadducee

The second largest religious group in Judea after the Pharisees, these Jewish leaders arose between the time of the return of the exiles to Jerusalem and the first century A.D. The Sadducees accepted the Law of Moses (first five books of the OT) but did not believe in a bodily resurrection, angels, or spirits.

Salvation

This word can be used in a general sense to describe the deliverance from an enemy, or in a more specific, technical sense to describe God's act of delivering people from their sin. This latter sense has both a partial fulfillment (by faith, now, in time) during what we are calling Rescue and Renewal as well as a complete, ultimate fulfillment on the Last Day.

Samaritan

During the divided kingdom following the death of Solomon, the northern tribes began to develop strict boundaries that included their own central place of worship on Mt. Gerizim to rival the southern temple in Jerusalem. After the northern tribes were captured and taken into exile, the Assyrians repopulated the region with people who had been conquered from other countries. This mixed group came to be known as the Samaritans after the place name Samaria. In the NT period this group was despised by the Jews, who traced their allegiance to the temple in Jerusalem.

Satan

A word that means "adversary" and is found first (chronologically) in the biblical record in the first and second chapters of Job. This word Satan refers to the archenemy of God and his creation. While the proper name is not used in the third chapter of Genesis, the biblical writers clearly identify the serpent as Satan (see also Jude 6 and Revelation 12:9).

Scribe

There were scribes during the OT period who copied the Scriptures to preserve God's Word for succeeding generations. By the NT period, however, this group had become a clearly identifiable subgroup among Jewish leaders.

Septuagint

This is the Latin name given to the Greek translation of the Hebrew OT. The Septuagint (often referenced by the Roman numerals LXX) was produced by Jews during the second century B.C., following the Hellenizing campaigns of Alexander the

Great. Younger generations increasingly lost Hebrew as their primary language and thus needed a Greek translation to learn the stories of the Bible.

Servant

This word is most closely associated with the writings of Isaiah the prophet. In his great work we hear about a servant who suffers (the Suffering Servant) on behalf of God's people. While there are five servant "songs" in Isaiah, the most familiar one comes from chapter 53.

Son

A term of endearment, first used by God in the OT to describe his relationship to his people, Israel, as a father to a son. Starting with the promise in Genesis 3:15, however, there is a narrow use of this word in the OT to describe the Messiah who would come in the person of Jesus. Son is the primary designation for the second person of the Trinity.

Son of David

This title is used for the heirs who followed the reign of David as king such as Solomon and Jeroboam. The people of Israel maintained the expectation that Yahweh would ultimately place an heir of David upon the throne in Jerusalem. The NT applies this title to Jesus as the fulfillment of God's promise.

Son of God

This is one of the NT designations for Jesus that emphasizes his full divinity.

Son of Man

This is one of the designations for Jesus that emphasizes his full humanity. Such is also the most common way that Jesus referenced himself, in the third person, as an echo of Daniel 7.

Space

A philosophical term that denotes places marked by limits and boundaries. From a theological perspective, God has revealed himself as unbound and limitless, although he willfully condescends to make himself known to human beings.

Special Revelation

This term is used in distinction from General (or Natural) Revelation. Special Revelation specifically refers to what God reveals about himself in the Bible that could not be known from any other source. For example, it is an historical fact that a man named Jesus suffered and died on a cross. We need the Bible, however, to explain that Jesus did this to atone for our sins.

Spiritual

This word is used to describe the "hidden" or mysterious work of God within his creation. While the Spirit cannot be seen with the human eye, he is nonetheless present and active.

Scripture

This word is used to designate the entire OT and NT. Prior to the NT being written down, Jesus frequently referred to the OT as the Scriptures. In 2 Timothy 3:16 we are told that "All Scripture is breathed out by God" and thus to be equated with God's Word.

Suffering

The trials, hardship, pain, and death that characterize the time between the Fall and Ultimate Restoration. Prior to the Fall, God's good creation did not include suffering, nor will such be present for those who have faith in Christ on the Last Day.

Synagogue

In general, this OT word means "to gather together," while the more specific use is found in the NT and refers to a Jewish place of worship. Christians eventually opted to use the word church ("called out ones") to describe their assemblies.

Synoptic Gospels

Synoptic is made up of two words (syn = with or together, and optic = to see) that simply mean "to see with or together." This term is a modern way of designating the first three Gospel accounts, namely, Matthew, Mark, and Luke, because they share a large amount of similar material. John is generally treated as later and somewhat supplementary to the other three.

Tabernacle and Temple

The Tabernacle, also called the "tent of meeting," was first introduced by Yahweh to Moses as a prescribed place of portable worship to be used during the wilderness wanderings. The Temple, on the other hand, was largely patterned after the Tabernacle, but was a permanent structure and place of worship constructed under the reign of Solomon in Jerusalem. The Temple that Jesus visited during his earthly ministry was the second Temple, which was constructed following the Babylonian Exile and expanded upon by Herod beginning in 20–19 B.C.

Testament

From the Latin *testamentum*, this word translates a Greek word in the NT that can also be translated with the word "covenant." Over the years, the word "testament" has often been used to describe the promise of salvation that Jesus gives as part of his "last will and testament." In more recent years, however, there has been a growing practice of using the word "covenant" as a way to demonstrate the consistent work of God on behalf of his creation throughout both OT and NT, which also requires the shedding of blood (the Hebrew literally says "to cut a covenant"). I have chosen the word "covenant" to describe the work of God, while retaining "testament" as a reference to the writings, both OT and NT.

The Angel of the Lord

This singular angel, marked by the use of the definite article "the," is distinguished in the OT from the hosts of heaven, or plurality of angels. Because this particular angel consistently speaks as God himself, and is described with qualities only attributable to God (especially as the source of "redemption"), it has become a practice by many to identify this angel with the second person of the Trinity, namely, Jesus as the messenger of God in his preincarnate glory. This is the position carried forward in this book.

Theology

Made up of two words, *theos* = God and *logos* = word/study of, theology simply means the study of God. More specifically, theology is the study of how God has chosen to reveal himself through his own word/s.

Time

A form of measurement, designed by God in his work of creation, to show purposeful, linear movement from one season and generation to the next.

Timeline

A way of talking about the metanarrative (or grand, overarching story) that God has constructed to bring his creation from its beginning to a complete and ultimate restoration. Everything that we read in Scripture can be understood most clearly in its relation to this grand story or Timeline.

Transcendent

Theologically, a way of talking about Yahweh as distinct from his creation. God is above and beyond his creation and not a created being himself. (Compare with Immanent.)

Trinity

From the Latin *trinitas*, which means "a set of three." While this word is not found in the Bible in reference to God, the concept certainly is. Theologically, this word is used to describe the nature of God as being three persons in one God, not three gods or only one person. (See the Nicene Creed.)

Truth

A philosophical (ethical) category that was first introduced, implicitly, when God commanded Adam and Eve to eat from the tree of life and live, but not to eat from the tree of the knowledge of good and evil, "for in that day you will surely die." When Satan tempted Eve to be like God by eating from the forbidden tree, this dialog highlighted the distinction between truth and falsehood.

Two Natures of Christ

A foundational teaching about Jesus is that he is both fully human (Son of Man) and fully divine (Son of God). Historically, the church has considered this teaching as central to the Christian faith (see Nicene Creed) and, thus, has underscored the necessity of the virgin birth (born of a woman and born of the Holy Spirit). For the purpose of salvation, Jesus had to be fully human so that he could live, suffer, and die in our place. He also had to be fully divine so that his life would be without sin, his death would be for all people, and he could rise from the dead with victory over Satan, sin, and death.

Type/Antitype

The Apostle Paul employs the word *typos* in Romans 5:14 to interpret how Adam prefigured or foreshadowed (type) the Second Adam, namely, Jesus (antitype). Theologians use the language of type and antitype to describe how people and events in the OT foreshadow the person and work of Christ in the NT.

Ultimate Restoration

This phrase is used to designate the second coming or appearing of Christ on the Last Day, when the final and complete reversal of God's fallen creation will be ultimately realized. (See Now, Not Yet.)

Word

The spoken and written word as found in what we call the OT and NT. The singular form was often used by the prophets to refer to an entire body of instruction/promise/warning from God.

Worship

This translates a word (and concept) found in both OT and NT that means "service." There are two sides or directions in worship, namely, the sacramental and the sacrificial side. The sacramental side is what God does for human beings such as rescue and renew them, while the sacrificial side is a person's (or, corporately, a people's) response to all that God has done on his/their behalf. Examples of sacrificial responses include tithes and offerings, service to God and others, as well as prayer and praise.

Yahweh

This is the personal name for God, first used in Genesis 2:4 alongside of the general word for God. Together, these two words are usually translated into English as "Lord [Yahweh] God." When God appeared to Moses in the burning bush, he reintroduced his personal name, Yahweh, because it had evidently fallen out of disuse (Exodus 3:13–14). The name Yahweh literally means "I am who I am," which speaks to the Lord's unique, eternal nature. He even commands Moses to tell the people in Egypt, "I Am has sent me." (Later Jesus picks up on this name when he speaks the great "I am" statements, especially as found in John chapters 10 and 14.)